The Princess Within

— FOR TEENS —

DISCOVERING YOUR ROYAL INHERITANCE

SERITA ANN JAKES

BETHANY HOUSE PUBLISHERS
a division of Baker Publishing Group
Minneapolis, Minnesota

Published by Bethany House Publishers
11400 Hampshire Avenue South
Bloomington, Minnesota 55438
www.bethanyhouse.com

Bethany House Publishers is a division of
Baker Publishing Group, Grand Rapids, Michigan

Printed in the United States of America

Library of Congress Cataloging-in-Publication Data
Jakes, Serita Ann.
    The princess within for teens : discovering your royal inheritance / Serita Ann
Jakes.
        pages cm
    Summary: "An adaptation for teen girls of the The Princess Within, the author
mentors young women giving them hope and an understanding of their journey to
wholeness"— Provided by publisher.
    ISBN 978-0-7642-1204-8 (pbk. : alk. paper)
    1. Teenage girls—Religious life. 2. Teenage girls—Conduct of life. 3. Christian
teenagers—Religious life. 4. Christian teenagers—Conduct of life. I. Title.
BV4551.3.J35 2014
248.8'33—dc23   2014006618

Cover design by Kirk DouPonce, DogEared Design

Author photograph by Rance Elgin Photography

Author is represented by Dupree/Miller & Associates

Manuscript prepared by Linda Washington

In keeping with biblical principles of creation stewardship, Baker Publishing Group advocates the responsible use of our natural resources. As a member of the Green Press Initiative, our company uses recycled paper when possible. The text paper of this book is composed in part of post-consumer waste.

14   15   16   17   18   19   20   7   6   5   4   3   2   1

Inside every little girl there is a woman
Inside every woman there is a little girl
This book is dedicated to US ALL

Contents

CONTENTS

Letters From My Daughters

Hey, Little Princess,

There is a woman inside of every girl, and a girl inside every woman. As you grow into what God has for you, it can be difficult to know how to really find who you are. This book is going to help you reach the person God plans for you to be.

Communication with your mother is essential in getting you to the place God has for you. When I was a little girl, my mom would give us little purses, and she would say, "Walk like Mommy." My sister and I would get behind her and mimic walking like her. She had such a soft voice, and we would mimic that too. I can remember seeing what my mommy wore and loving it, and asking her, "Do they have that in little-girl size?" My whole life, even still now, I have watched my mom and tried to emulate the class that she carried.

When you are a teenager, learning new things about your body and discovering who you are, there is no manual to teach you how to find the princess within. There is no manual to show you how to become a lady. My mother has always had a heart for little women, and I am thrilled that she has taken her heart and placed it in words for you. She has given you the opportunity—and the manual—to find the princess within you.

In life, you will go through things, but it is important for you to know that your purpose and destiny are resting on the inside of you. This book is going to help you pull out that destiny and purpose.

My mother used to sit my sister and me down and talk about how to take care of ourselves and our bodies and to just love ourselves as the princesses we truly are. This book is just that: She is sitting down and sharing her heart with you, just as she did with my sister and me.

There is so much waiting on the inside of you and developing on the inside of you. You are stronger than you know and brighter than you know. This book is simply going to share with you how to tap into that. I believe after so many years we have waited for a manual to tap into the lady God has chosen us to be even at a young age, and this is your manual. I am so happy that you finally have a key, and even more excited to see you step into your destiny. Wishing you the best as you learn how to be all that you can be, and as you truly discover the princess within.

Your Big Sister,
Cora Coleman

Dear Little Sister,

When I was your age, I was so unsure of who I was. I wanted so badly to be understood by others, or at least by myself. Why did I feel the way I did? I remember hearing people tell me often that I was special. They had no idea I felt anything but special! My differences made me insecure until it made me desperate for attention. I wanted to hide behind the concept of normal, where no one else would see my truth. Now, a bit older, I want to share a tip with you before you read this book:

Open your heart.

Don't read this looking for all the ways it doesn't apply to you because "you're different." For a moment just give in to the idea that someone may understand exactly how you feel. The truth is that throughout your life there will be moments when you question who you are. You will wonder why it's so easy for others to feel comfortable in their own skin while you struggle. Those moments don't go away easily. For many of our sisters, those thoughts convinced them to settle for less than God's best. I have been there.

I learned a valuable lesson in those times.

It may not always be easy to fully love yourself in the face of many uncertainties, but it is rewarding. I feel as though it's the secret polish that allows our crowns to fully shine. When we begin to love the smallest details from our crooked smiles to our secret tears, the fullness of God's light can shine upon us. Believe me, I know, it's much easier said than done. That's why your heart must be open to this change. Grace insists we quiet our self-doubt and give voice to God in us. Fear cannot reside where love abides. Allow the sincerity of words in this book to echo into the depths of your heart.

I can't imagine a woman more fitting to shed light on discovering the royalty that exists in us all than my mother. She is consistently honest and courageously gentle as she empowers us to show love in the face of pain. Countless times I've witnessed her choosing love in the face of fear. The seeds God has given her to plant restoration, hope, and determination in women have a harvest well into the millions. My sister and I, however, had the honor of being in her heart's garden. We have been witnesses to many seasons in her life—some of sadness and many of joy. Yet I've never seen her cave into the pressure to abandon who she is. I used to wonder whether she was birthed with such incredible resilience or learned to be loyal to her truth through heartache.

Then I realized that what was more important than how she learned it was who her teacher was. She learned from the ultimate Master. It humbles me that He thought enough of me to allow me to dwell in her heart as well. This book, another labor of love, will produce seeds in your life for many years to come.

Open your heart, princess. It's time to shine!

Sarah Jakes

Acknowledgments

From my earliest years of existence, I have been taught to always express gratitude to those who have been kind to me, supported my endeavors, and valued me as an individual.

While writing my first book, *The Princess Within*, I was awe-inspired by those who encouraged me to share my diary as written to my "Secret Keeper." My gratefulness overflowed from a sincere heart. Almost fifteen years later, I find myself penning words of sincere appreciation to all who thought that it was time for me to speak into the lives of young girls, "There is a princess inside of you!"

My unlocked diary would have been buried in the drawer without the nudging of my literary agency, Dupree/Miller & Associates, and publisher, Bethany House, and without the creative anointing of Linda Washington. TDJ Enterprises, thank you for lending me your chariot.

The diary pages would have yellowed with my generation had I not dared to launch The Potter's House of Dallas's ministry Distinctively Debutantes. You've added significance to the autumn of my life.

My husband, Bishop T.D. Jakes Sr., always know that you inspired me to walk with dignity and as an heiress to the precious promises of God.

My sons, Jamar, Jemaine, and Dexter Jr., you all are destined and will reign over every obstacle that would suggest defeat.

My daughters, Cora and Sarah, walk like Mommy . . . as she walks with God.

May my grandchildren ever know that as their Granny passed this way, her God will become their God too.

Well, Secret Keeper, You already know everything that I have whispered in Your ear. Thank You for holding me until all of my fears subside, heavenly Father. What a coronation!

Your Life:
A Fairy Tale in the Making

You've probably watched at least a few Disney princess movies over the years, right? Which Disney princess are you like? Belle (*Beauty and the Beast*), Cinderella (*Cinderella*), Merida (*Brave*), Mulan (*Mulan*), or Tiana (*The Princess and the Frog*)? Take this personality quiz to find out.

1. You get invited to the biggest party ever, which will take place in two weeks. You don't have a thing to wear, though. So you . . .
   a. Babysit or work some other part-time job(s) to earn money.
   b. Sigh and say you can't go.
   c. Borrow an outfit.
   d. Look up a pattern in a book or on the Internet and make an awesome outfit.
   e. Go in your most comfortable clothes and dare anyone to say anything.

2. You hear that the hottest guy at school has asked your BFF about you. You . . .
   a. Tell your BFF to tell him you're too focused on work and school to date anyone right now.
   b. Doubt that anyone that cool would be interested in you.
   c. Ignore what he said until he proves himself.
   d. Would go out with him if he's smart and fun to be around.
   e. Challenge him in the sport you excel at to see if he's worthy of you.

3. Most people would describe you as . . .
   a. A hard worker.
   b. Too shy for your own good.
   c. An ingenious risk taker.
   d. A bookworm.
   e. Headstrong and totally against the status quo.

4. You need money for college, so you . . .
   a. Strive to get good grades to get a scholarship, but work during the school year and every summer to save as much as you can.
   b. Strive to get good grades to get a scholarship, but consider going to a community college for a year if things don't work out.
   c. Figure out a way to get the college of your choice to give you a scholarship.
   d. Strive for a perfect score on the SAT or ACT, since you already have good grades.
   e. Take a year off to travel after high school until you can decide if college is what you really want.

5. When others disagree with you, you . . .
   a. Tell them about their faults.
   b. Wind up taking their side.

    c. Try to help them see your side of things.

    d. Stand up for what you believe, but are willing to compromise.

    e. Try to prove them wrong.

6. When facing an impossible task, you . . .

    a. Work even harder.

    b. Hope that someone comes along to help you.

    c. Figure out a clever way to solve it.

    d. Break the task into smaller goals you can easily reach.

    e. Find a way to work around it somehow.

7. When it comes to family, you . . .

    a. Are close to them.

    b. Aren't very close.

    c. Would take any risk to help them.

    d. Take care of them.

    e. Argue a lot, but when it comes down to it, you love them.

If you answered mostly As, you're like Tiana—you're willing to work hard to reach any goal.

If you answered mostly Bs, you're like Cinderella—sweet, but doubtful of your own strengths.

If you answered mostly Cs, you're like Mulan—you like to figure things out. You're the girl with the plan!

If you answered mostly Ds, you're like Belle—confident, into the books, but love to have fun too.

If you answered mostly Es, you're like Merida—you're willing to take a stand for what you believe is right. You want to chart your own path.

If you have a mixture of answers, you're like many teens. You have your moments of confidence and moments of doubt.

In each of these movies, the heroine solves her problems in two hours and lives happily ever after. In some cases, a magic wand is waved and *poof*—problem solved. Wouldn't it be great if life were that easy? But life often is anything *but* easy. It's often messy and complicated. Maybe it's that way for you right now. Instead of the fairy tale, it is a horror story with no escape. Perhaps you've gone through heartache after heartache with no end in sight.

There's good news: Unlike the heroines of horror stories, who are often alone and victimized, you are not alone. God is with you. He designed you to be a princess, to live happily ever after. If you find that difficult to believe, especially when you face problem after problem, keep reading, my young sister. I wrote this book for you to remind you that you aren't powerless, but *powerful*, thanks to your heavenly Father—the King of the Universe.

The story of Cinderella and her glass slipper, meeting a handsome prince who falls in love with her, isn't just a fairy tale. It's your story and my story—only not exactly told the way Disney tells it. I'll explain more, so keep reading.

In each chapter you'll find a short story lead-in—the Cinderella story updated for today (I'm calling her Ella) and told in parts—and a suggested playlist to inspire you, followed by a discussion on various topics that affect teens (social media, relationships, school, eating disorders, abuse), quizzes or questions, and a real-life story. Closing each chapter is a mini-devotional ("What's your story?") with questions to answer to help you meet with the God who cares so much about you.

At the end of the book, you'll find a section called "What You Need to Know About . . ." that provides information on topics like salvation and baptism. Plus, there is a handy resources section with websites, phone numbers, and other contact information, if you need help. At the end of the book are great passages of Scripture you can read when you feel alone, sad, or powerless.

It's time for you to discover that dreams really do come true with an all-powerful God in your corner. With God, you are a princess.

Love,
Serita Ann

My Story

A "princess of God" sounds like a girl or a young lady who has a desire to strengthen her Christian relationship with God. She is known for her Christian character in how she treats and respects others. As a princess, she is pressured to view herself as separated from secular influences because she is special. The princess doesn't always live up to those expectations. As a princess, she still strives to learn from her mistakes, has unyielding faith and courage, and works toward accomplishing her goals in life.

As God's princess, she is separated from the secular influences of the world to reach God's higher calling for her life. God has a greater purpose and plan in store for her.

Kennedy

CHAPTER 1

Princess, Why Are You Hiding?

Life is like a fairy tale. . . .

Ella kept a to-do list on her phone a mile long. School. Homework. Chores. After school job. She had forgotten what it was like to live differently. But keeping busy was the best way to forget about what happened. If only she could forget how Josh had made a fool of her, then posted the results all over Facebook.

Her friends texted constantly. *Where r u? Come b w/ us.* They were trying at least. But hang out? In public? And be humiliated? No thank you! Even thinking about what had happened was painful.

PLAYLIST

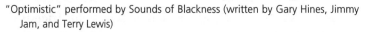

"Optimistic" performed by Sounds of Blackness (written by Gary Hines, Jimmy Jam, and Terry Lewis)

"Perfect People" performed by The Walls Group (written by Kirk Franklin)

Tempted to hide?

Once upon a time, there was a girl named Ella. She was just like you—she went to school and had friends and a family. But some of her problems had to do with family and friends. Her home life wasn't great. I'll tell you more about that in the chapters ahead. And a friend hurt her deeply. So she tried to hide away from everyone by keeping herself busy.

Does that tactic sound familiar? Let's talk about the secrets that cause people to hide.

Social media make us all mini-celebrities, thanks to photos splashed across the computer screen, shared videos, and status updates available for all of our friends to see.

Many people crave the fifteen minutes of fame that Andy Warhol, an internationally famous painter, claimed that everyone would one day have. But the downside of being a celebrity is the fact that mistakes are often put on public display. Photos are taken and videos are made and watched over and over with comments enabled for the public to weigh in. After all, who hasn't seen videos of "wardrobe mishaps" or celebrity mug shots after run-ins with the law?

But let's talk about the average teen. Many are tempted to hide when others post negative messages about them on Facebook and other social media, or a boyfriend changes his status from "in a relationship" to "single"—the way to break up with someone. Suddenly, the Facebook timeline becomes a wall of shame that others can access.

Some teens might be tempted to hide because they've allowed a boyfriend to take compromising pictures (or they took the pictures themselves), which he then sent to his friends or shared with others through Instagram or Snapchat. Or perhaps damaging lies were tweeted and repeated or sexting messages they thought were private were leaked all over school. Has that ever happened to you or to someone you know?

Shameful secrets make us afraid to show our faces in public. We withdraw in fear that someone will bring our experience to the knowledge of others. Intimidation is a dark and dreary place in which to live. Even when light penetrates our room, we look for dark corners to retreat to so we can keep our secrets from exposure.

The sad thing is that hiding becomes almost impossible the more you live your life through social media. An article at VanityFair.com, "Friends Without Benefits," written by Nancy Jo Sales, included this snippet of a conversation:

> "Social media is destroying our lives," said the girl at the Grove.
> "So why don't you go off it?" I asked.
> "Because then we would have no life," said her friend.[1]

Would you agree?

A trusted secret keeper

Hiding feels comfortable at the time, but it is a lonely lifestyle to maintain. If secrets are allowed to run the course of their destruction, finding new ways to keep these secrets can become more sacred than our search for freedom from them. There is hope, however, for people who find a trustworthy friend to whom they can tell their secrets. Many people have found healing by revealing their secrets to a person who can demonstrate forgiveness to them. Secrets lose their power if there is no longer a reason to hide their truths. The right secret keeper can make the person feel acceptable again.

This need for the acceptance of others drives us to great measures, because we tend to agree with the opinions that others have of us. If our peers want to imitate us, we are flattered. If they make fun of us, we are defeated. That's why we must be careful who we choose to be our secret keeper. If we tell our secret to the wrong person, he or she might use it against us and inflict more shame on us than we previously carried. But it is also true that if we share a secret with someone who accepts us for the new person in Christ that we are becoming, we find liberation from our guilt and enjoy new beginnings.

The secret ingredient is love

Do your friends tell you their secrets? I guard the secrets of those who confide in me. It is my way of showing them that I accept them as they are. My belief in them helps to relieve their sense of shame as they accept my love in spite of what has happened to them or what they have done. I am not so much concerned about the choices they made in their past but in the choices they will make in the future.

I learned this art of secret keeping from God, who has been faithful to keep my secrets—secrets that kept me from enjoying the new life He gave to me. He accepts me, so I can accept others.

Think of the last secret you had. Maybe it was something you didn't want anyone to know about you. Now think about how you felt. Alone? Afraid? Ashamed? Secrets rob us of the freedom and joy we can have in life. They rob us *of* life. Think about the people you know who seem like they're carrying a great load. They're probably quieter than they usually are. Maybe you don't see them as often. They don't act the way they usually act.

Some people pretend they're not in pain, preferring to hide behind a fake smile. I've kept a smile pasted on my face even when I've been in pain. I was afraid of my future because of my past. But I found a secret weapon.

My secret weapon

I met my Lord, my Secret Keeper. Once I gave to Him the secrets that kept me from being totally His, I found that those same secrets were now totally His to keep. He removed the shame that I felt and covered me with His truth and love again. Thanks to His love, I have nothing to hide.

I have found healing by writing letters to the Lord, my Secret Keeper. Have you ever felt really, really peaceful? The act of explaining my fears and waiting for God to answer gave me peace. Writing to Him caused me to be still and to listen to Him.

When I was a teen, I wanted to hide because of the shame I felt. You see, I had this boyfriend who rejected me. His actions toward me made me feel unlovely and unwanted.

It took a while, but I had to get real before God and admit my secret pain to Him. I wrote,

Dear Secret Keeper,

It was right after my brother died. No, let me correct that statement. It was right after my brother was murdered. My whole world seemed to come to a screeching halt. How could his life be ended so abruptly, just when he was trying to get it all together? He had given his life to You. For the first time in his life, my brother seemed to have found true happiness—the kind of happiness that I knew (even then) only came from having You as the center of his life.

One evening he went out with his daughters to one of the local hangouts. The girls were raising money for a trip to an amusement park, and their daddy was taking them

where all of his friends would be. Everybody liked my brother, I thought. But something went wrong. There was an argument. Then there were gunshots, and my brother tumbled to the bottom of the stairs.

Oh, Secret Keeper, I was looking for someone who enjoyed having fun like my brother. I thought I found someone like that. My boyfriend liked to have fun, but sometimes he seemed so angry. I began to notice bouts of anger that soon became hostility toward me. The hostility turned into verbal outbursts that I could not believe my ears were hearing. As suddenly as it happened, he would return to being the person I had grown so fond of.

He visited every day. I even recognized the sound of his car when he drove up. But the visits became shorter; there was always something else he had to do. As the visits grew briefer, the atmosphere became more intense and often resulted in senseless arguments. I felt like something wasn't right. I could almost sense danger every time he came.

In my heart, I felt warned that the relationship was taking a turn for the worse. The accusations turned into rage. The rage turned into threats of violence. What game was this we played?

My Secret Keeper helped me with His Word: Psalm 121:1–8. I looked up the Scripture and read it to myself as though the Lord were speaking it directly to me:

Dear Serita Ann,

You will lift up your eyes to the hills—where does your help come from? Your help comes from me, the Lord, the Maker of heaven and earth.

I will not let your foot slip—I who watch over you will not slumber; indeed, I who watch over Israel will neither slumber nor sleep. I, the Lord, watch over you—I am your shade at your right hand; the sun will not harm you by day, nor the moon by night.

I, the Lord, will keep you from all harm—I will watch over your life; I, the Lord, will watch over your coming and going both now and forevermore.

I returned to my writing and finished telling my Lord the secret that had haunted me.

I don't know why I didn't heed the warning that You gave to me. I knew that things were about to come to a boil. Whenever I heard his car, I became nervous. It had been nearly a week. There had been neither phone calls nor visits. If history was to be repeated, I knew that when he did return he would be very hateful.

The day my boyfriend returned was an awful day. He made me feel ashamed for being me. I relived the day in my letter to my Secret Keeper:

It sounds like the car has stopped. Why is he walking so fast? Oh please, no arguing again. "But I haven't been anywhere!" I remember saying.

It hurts when he shoves like this.

Why is he pushing me?

Is that a gun in his hand?

What is he doing?

I've never seen such a face; it's like looking at the devil himself. Is he going to kill me, Secret Keeper? He's got his gun to my head, and I'm lying on the floor. God, help me!

But God spared my life:

I looked up and he was gone. I crawled to the window and peeked under the shade. He stood there beneath the full moon, cocked the gun, and fired it into the air five times. I sat on the floor trembling; tears would not come. Everything that I thought he was had turned to lies. When I met him, I felt so lonely. When he drove off, again I felt left alone.

But then I realized that I had not been left alone. I had called out to You, and You had sent an angel to rescue me from death! I'm never alone because I always have You, Secret Keeper.

Love,
Serita Ann

Because of the way he treated me, I thought I deserved to be treated disrespectfully. He had stripped me of my sense of self-worth and had robbed me of my dignity. But now, after laying my secret before the Lord, after wrestling with the truth that God was there protecting me and saving me from further harm, I no longer felt ashamed.

Why do we keep our secrets to ourselves instead of giving them to God, our Secret Keeper and trusted friend? With Jesus we can come out of hiding.

WHAT'S *your* STORY?

Writing out your feelings will help you to see what God already knows about you. So why not write a letter to the Lord, your Secret Keeper, in your journal? Each time you write, tell Him what secret makes you want to hide.

To get you started, read the passage below. From what troubles do you want God to save you?

This poor man called, and the Lord heard him; he saved him out of all his troubles. The angel of the Lord encamps around those who fear him, and he delivers them.

Psalm 34:6–7

Ask God what He thinks about your secret. Then listen to His still, small voice within your heart and record His response in your journal or below.

CHAPTER 2

But Everyone Is Invited!

Life is like a fairy tale. . . .

When Ella checked her email, her mouth dropped open. An Evite to a ball lay in her inbox. Her eyes weren't playing tricks on her!

Not just any ball. One given in honor of a visiting prince—an actual prince.

Every girl her age was invited—that's what the Evite said. She checked a few of her friends' Facebook timelines. They were invited too. Even her stepsisters—Olivia and Marilla—tweeted about being invited.

Ella returned to the Evite, reading it once more. But how could she go? What if the prince didn't like the way she looked? What if he found out about her public humiliation? Would he take back his invitation?

PLAYLIST

"Invitation" performed by Byron Cage (written by Alex Williams)

"Show Me" performed by Yolanda Adams (written by Kirk Franklin)

"God Will Take Care of You" performed by Le'Andria Johnson (written by Civilla D. Martin)

Left out

Parties, coffeehouse hangouts, the mall, dinner at restaurants, vacations, strolls along the lake—it's nice to be invited to fun events and places, isn't it? It's even nicer when your friends are invited too. For some events, the more the merrier.

Have you ever learned of a party that an acquaintance was hosting, but you didn't know for sure if you were invited? Perhaps a general announcement was made at school or on Facebook, but you didn't get the Evite. When your friends asked if you were going, you were too embarrassed to admit that you didn't think you were on the guest list, so you just said, "No, I'm not going." Or maybe you were too proud to find out for sure if you were to be included, so you played it off by announcing that you had plans for that day.

But perhaps there was a time when you weren't invited to an event that you wished you *could* attend. What's worse is that *your friends* were invited. When you discover that you've been excluded, what do you usually do?

a. Tell your friend to boycott the event.

b. Cry and mope.

c. Get mad and spread rumors on Facebook about the person who excluded you.

d. Plan your own event for the same day and invite your friends.

e. Pray about it.

f. Other: _____.

No one likes to feel left out. But sometimes we feel that way because we think we don't measure up in some way (looks, talent, intelligence, money, popularity, etc.). When we play the comparison game with others, someone always loses, especially when we think any of those factors makes a person more deserving of inclusion.

God looks at each of us as if we were His only daughter. And of course, He always wants us to be included in all He is doing. But people are not always like God. They sometimes deliberately exclude others.

Weighty matters

Feeling left out can fill us with a sense of shame. It's difficult to admit that we feel hurt when we're left out, so we keep our pain of being excluded a secret. But that's like living in denial. What would happen if we told our Secret Keeper how we felt? What would He say to us if we would quiet ourselves before Him after admitting our shame to Him?

I have felt left out before, so I wrote to my Lord, my Secret Keeper:

Dear Secret Keeper,

Even as a child, I learned that insensitive remarks inflict pain. I often felt that I was the target of most of the darts of humiliation. I can still feel some of the pain from those who would chant, "Fatty, fatty, two-by-four!" These were the children I wanted most to impress. I wasn't athletic, but was forever trying to be selected for the neighborhood sporting events. My dresses often looked like they were designed for someone much older because the chubby selections of the mail order catalogs were very limited.

In my eyes, everyone looked like they could model for Seventeen *magazine. They all were tall with long legs— unlike me, who was the runt of the litter and as wide as I was tall. No one would accept me but my mama, who indulged me with her sweet potato pies and chocolate cakes. She understood that I was a growing girl.*

I thought the other girls who had called me names were so beautiful. Somehow they were the epitome of all I ever hoped to be—thin.

Maybe you can relate to my pain. One of the biggest reasons people turn down invitations is the fear of how they might look to others. Negative body image is a struggle for many teens. The issue of weight is one of the prime factors in the fight against a healthy body image. A study in 2010 found that more than one-third of children and adolescents were overweight or obese.[1] Many are teased or bullied, which adds to their sense of shame.

Negative body image comes out in other ways, namely eating disorders like anorexia nervosa, bulimia nervosa, or binge eating. Perhaps you know someone who struggles with an eating disorder. Could that person be you?

Good Morning America discussed "thigh gap"—the gap a girl has between her thighs when she's standing up—and how many teen girls are obsessed with whether theirs are wide enough. Teens interviewed for the story mentioned pictures girls posted of themselves on Instagram, Facebook, and Tumblr and the pressure to maintain "thigh gap." If you don't have the ideal amount of thigh gap, you don't, as the reporter intoned, "measure up."[2]

Thanks to social media, everyone's watching and comparing themselves with others. In fact, a teen's likelihood of developing an eating disorder increases as time spent on social media increases.[3]

Over half a million teens admit to an eating disorder, according to the National Eating Disorders Association. Since 1930, each decade has seen a rise in incidents of anorexia in young women between the ages of fifteen and nineteen.[4]

Sad statistics, aren't they? But for many, they are a sad reality. Negative body image? That's life and no way out—according to some.

God's image of you

In chapter 5 I'll talk more about body image. For now, let's take a look at this passage from Psalm 139, written by David—former shepherd, giant slayer, and king:

> For You formed my inward parts; You covered me in my mother's womb. I will praise You, for I am fearfully and wonderfully made; marvelous are Your works, and that my soul knows very well. My frame was not hidden from You, when I was made in secret, and skillfully wrought in the lowest parts of the earth.
>
> Psalm 139:13–15 NKJV

Like David, do you believe that you are "fearfully and wonderfully made"? Or do you doubt that you were "skillfully wrought" by God? If you have a hard time believing that skill wrought you, consider this: God crafted you with unimaginable tenderness. To Him you're a priceless jewel, even if you have a hard time believing it.

I wrote a letter to my Secret Keeper about my own view.

Dear Secret Keeper,

You continually look beyond my flaws and meet my needs. Now when I look for a role model or someone to imitate, I look into the mirror of Your Word. I behold palely the image that You are creating, and I shed secret tears because I can hardly believe that this is how You see me.

Little sister, you were made in the image of God (Genesis 1:26–27). God gave you some of His characteristics (love, creativity, joy) and His ability to relate to others. That means you are a wonderful creation. Believe it!

WHAT'S *your* STORY?

What's your usual response to problems? Do you try to handle everything yourself? Or do you seek help? Read the passage below. Jesus spoke these words. Consider them your invitation to come to Him with the worries you have. Journal about them. Give them all to Him. Then listen to His still, small voice within your heart and record His response in your journal. (If you don't know Jesus as your Savior, check out pages 185–190 to learn how you can.)

> Come to Me, all you who labor and are heavy laden, and I will give you rest. Take My yoke upon you and learn from Me, for I am gentle and lowly in heart, and you will find rest for your souls. For My yoke is easy and My burden is light
>
> Matthew 11:28–30 NKJV

What would "rest for your soul" look like for you? Write about it or talk about it in prayer.

CHAPTER 3

Parents Just Don't Understand?

Life is like a fairy tale. . . .

"Girl, you've been on that computer all day."

When her stepmother took that tone, Ella knew an argument was coming. "I just got on it to check something," she said, trying to sound as pleasant as possible.

"Did you just roll your eyes at me? I *know* you're not rolling your eyes at me. Get off the computer. *Now.*"

Ella turned back to the screen, clicking away from her email.

"You've got chores to do. Get to them."

Ella counted to three, then quietly said, "Yes, ma'am."

PLAYLIST

"Never Would Have Made It" written and performed by Marvin Sapp

"Trust His Heart" written by Eddie Carswell and Babbie Mason

My parents just don't get it!

Could you have given the response Ella gave? Or would you have argued back? Have you ever had to bite your tongue to avoid giving lip to a parent or some other adult?

Years ago, the Fresh Prince—Will Smith—and DJ Jazzy Jeff made a video for their hit single "Parents Just Don't Understand." It's now considered a classic. In it, Will expresses what many teens think about parents and other adults: "Parents just don't understand!" Can you relate? Have you said similar words recently?

You may not believe this, but your parents probably said something similar to *their* parents. Each generation is certain that the older generation doesn't understand what life in the *now* is like. Music, clothes, free time, boyfriends—these are the great dividers, where opinions and reactions come fast and furious.

"Girl, I know you're not leaving this house wearing that!" "What's wrong with what I'm wearing?"

"Turn that racket down!" "You always complain about my music."

"Honey, I don't like Jeff." "But he loves me."

"Are you going to sit in front of the TV all day?" "Why do I have to *do* anything? Can't I just chill?"

Sometimes the lines of communication shut down when one side thinks the other side is totally out of touch. Has that happened in your family lately? Perhaps arguments have flared up due to your clothing or music preferences or because of other choices made recently. The communication gap widens as one side refuses to listen to the other. Soon, communication breaks down altogether.

At times like that, how would you react to a passage like this?

Children, obey your parents in the Lord, for this is right. "Honor your father and mother"—which is the first commandment with a promise—"so that it may go well with you and that you may enjoy long life on the earth."

Ephesians 6:1–3

Circle the statement that finishes the following sentence starter:

I feel . . .

a. Like screaming!
b. Indifferent. Adults always say stuff like that. And an adult wrote that, so . . .
c. Like I try my best to obey.
d. None of the above.

Yes, an adult—Paul the missionary and apostle of the first century—wrote that passage. However, he quoted from Exodus 20:12, where God established the command to obey parents. Did you know that back in Old Testament times, disobedience to parents could result in severe punishment—namely death?

They didn't get *Him* either

Sounds unfair? Before you stomp away from this book, let me share the story of a young man who could have said what Will Smith rapped: "Parents just don't understand."

Now his parents went to Jerusalem every year at the Feast of the Passover. And when he was twelve years old, they went up according to custom. And when the feast was ended, as they were returning, the boy Jesus stayed behind in Jerusalem. His parents did not know it, but supposing him to be in the group they went a day's journey, but then they began to search for him among their relatives and acquaintances, and when they did not find him, they returned to Jerusalem, searching for him. After three days they found him in the temple, sitting among the teachers, listening to them and asking them questions. And all who heard him were amazed at his understanding and his answers.

And when his parents saw him, they were astonished. And his mother said to him, "Son, why have you treated us so? Behold, your father and I have been searching for you in great distress."

And he said to them, "Why were you looking for me? Did you not know that I must be in my Father's house?" And they did not understand the saying that he spoke to them. And he went down with them and came to Nazareth and was submissive to them. And his mother treasured up all these things in her heart.

Luke 2:41–51 ESV

Read part of that last verse again: "And he went down with them and came to Nazareth and was submissive to them." Keep in mind that Jesus, before He came to earth as a baby, was the Creator, as John wrote in his gospel: "All things were made through him, and without him was not any thing made that was made" (John 1:3 ESV). But Jesus didn't come to earth to be the Boss. He came to be a servant:

Who, being in very nature God, did not consider equality with God something to be used to his own advantage; rather, he made himself nothing by taking the very nature of a servant, being made in human likeness.

Philippians 2:6–7

He also came to do things right. Knowing that obedience to His parents was a priority with God, He submitted to His parents.

Problem parents and other adults

You might be thinking, *Easy for* Him. *You don't know my pops or my mama!* Perhaps submitting to a parent or guardian is next to impossible for you, especially if that person has greatly wronged you. You wouldn't be alone either. Many teens have been verbally or physically abused by an alcoholic or drug-addled parent. And some parents have psychological issues, rendering them unstable and unfit parents.

According to the Bureau of Justice Statistics, between 1998 and 2002, violence against a son or daughter accounted for 11 percent of the 3.5 million violent crimes committed within families.[1] I can only imagine how those statistics have changed for the worse in an economy where tempers simmer and family members take out their frustration on one another.

Perhaps you don't have much of a relationship with a parent if he or she is currently in prison or absent for another reason. Perhaps the only parent you know is a grandparent or another older relative who was awarded custody of you. In the United States, almost 8 million children live with a grandparent—and for about 3 million of those kids, the grandparent is the primary caregiver.[2] Is that how life is for you?

Maybe the lack of communication at home isn't the issue. Perhaps you have a teacher who simply doesn't get you, or there's some other adult (the principal, an interviewer who seems to look down on you, a grumpy neighbor, the officer who pulls you over because you look "suspicious," a store owner who follows you around because he thinks you'll steal something) who doesn't like teens and seems out to get you. This just goes to show that we live in an imperfect world. Adults aren't always fair. Some who lack wise judgment are cruel.

So what's the solution if you have an adult like that in your life? What do you do if you have difficulty getting along with that person?

One solution is to keep the lines of communication open.

Communication solutions

Misunderstandings come when communication stops. With misunderstandings come hurt feelings, accusations, and stress. But if both sides are willing to compromise and work toward understanding, peace can result. Try these communication tips:

1. *Listen before you react*. When was the last time someone really listened to you? If you can recall that experience, try it with someone. When was the last time you asked your parent or guardian about his or her day? You could take the initiative and ask. Listening is one of the most loving things a person can do for someone else.

   Listening involves just that: listening. You can't talk and listen at the same time. Listening can also involve waiting until the person speaks and then reflecting back, in a non-sarcastic way, what he or she has said, even if what that person said is an accusation. This is an effective communication tool after a parent or some other adult scolds you about something. In that way, you show that you were listening. "So you want me to clean my room more." If you listen first, rather than reacting, you might discover an adult's willingness to give you the same courtesy of listening.

2. *Talk, rather than tune out*. I know you like your tunes and texting your friends. But if you want your parent or guardian to understand your perspective, you have to tune in and talk beyond "Yep," "Nope," and "Uh-huh." Maybe she's asking about your day because she really cares and wants to know what's going on.

3. *Try to speak respectfully*. When talking to someone in authority, try to watch your temper and your tone. It's difficult when someone has treated you wrongfully, I know. But smart-mouthing a police officer or the principal will only net you a world of trouble. Respect has to be earned.

4. *Pray.* God is the best communicator ever. He even interprets grunts! "In the same way, the Spirit helps us in our weakness. We do not know what we ought to pray for, but the Spirit himself intercedes for us through wordless groans" (Romans 8:26). You can tell God anything. He can handle anything you can dish out. He also knows your parent or guardian or that troublesome adult better than you know that person.

If, however, you're really being mistreated by an adult in authority, don't keep silent. Find someone you can trust and tell your story. If possible, provide documentation (for example, emails, letters, etc.) to back up your account.

You have a heavenly Parent

Even if you have a parent who bailed on you, you are not parentless. God is King of the Universe, but also a heavenly Father to those who have received new life through His Son, Jesus. The following verses assure you that God is your Father.

> But to all who did receive Him, He gave them the right to be children of God, to those who believe in His name.
>
> John 1:12 HCSB

> For if you forgive other people when they sin against you, your heavenly Father will also forgive you.
>
> Matthew 6:14

Ever get a guarantee for something? Perhaps you were guaranteed a spot on a team or guaranteed a scholarship. Well, the Holy Spirit is the guarantee that you belong to God. If He lives in you, that proves it.

> And you also were included in Christ when you heard the message of truth, the gospel of your salvation. When you believed, you

were marked in him with a seal, the promised Holy Spirit, who is a deposit guaranteeing our inheritance until the redemption of those who are God's possession—to the praise of his glory.

Ephesians 1:13–14

You can find more verses about God's love on page 186 in the section on salvation. Next time you feel alone, remember that your heavenly Father is always with you. Even if your parent or guardian does not understand, God always does.

WHAT'S *your* STORY?

Read the following verses. Just because you see them in the Bible, that doesn't mean that God isn't speaking them directly to you here . . . right now. Write a note to your Secret Keeper. What do you want to tell Him about your life? What do you think He understands or misunderstands? If you doubt whether He wants to hear from you, reread the first verse again and again.

The Lord appeared to us in the past, saying: "I have loved you with an everlasting love; I have drawn you with unfailing kindness."

Jeremiah 31:3

Grace and peace to you from God our Father and the Lord Jesus Christ.

Ephesians 1:2

Perhaps peace seems impossible because you're at war with God. If so, how did the war begin? Are you willing to talk to Him about how you feel?

CHAPTER 4

The Power to Choose

Life is like a fairy tale. . . .

The responses to the Evite poured in. Most fell under Yes. A few Maybes were listed. But no names appeared under No. Yet Ella's finger hovered over No. She couldn't make herself click it, however. Instead, she read some of the messages of those who had clicked Yes:

> Lookn 4wrd 2 it!
>
> Gonna get my flirt on!
>
> Getting a new dress!

A dress! She hadn't thought about it. She didn't have money for a dress, even if she chose to go. Her stepmother had plenty, though she never seemed to want to give Ella any to spend. In fact, her wallet with her credit cards was on the table nearby. Ella knew that her stepsisters sometimes "borrowed" their mother's credit card, then acted innocent when the bill came. Ella didn't think she'd have the nerve to do something like that. But what if she chose to look out for herself for a change like her stepsisters did? How different her life would be if she were more "in your face" like them, instead of shy and quiet.

PLAYLIST

"I Have Decided to Follow Jesus" performed by Third Day (written by Sundar Singh, later arranged by William Jensen Reynolds)

"Mighty to Save" written and performed by Ben Fielding and Reuben Morgan

Presto change-o

Ever see a chameleon? They use color as camouflage and also to let other chameleons know how they're feeling: "I'm angry" or "I'd like you to be my mate." Somehow they know what the color choices mean. ☺

Sometimes people act like chameleons. Some girls wear one outfit to school under the watchful eye of a parent, only to change their outfits to fit in at school. Some wear dark colors, hoping to blend in and not stand out. Others avoid certain colors, even if they are favorites, because they know these colors are gang colors and they want to avoid trouble.

Some teens try to change their personalities to fit in. Perhaps you've wished you had the ability to blend in with your surroundings. Or maybe you had a friend who totally changed her personality and ditched you for the popular crowd and now refuses to speak to you. Hurts, doesn't it?

Still others act a certain way (harder, more sarcastic) because they don't want others to think they're weak or religious. They fear being mocked.

The me nobody knows?

Reality shows like *Catfish* reveal how people treat the Internet as a place to start over—a place they can hide under a fake

43

persona complete with fake pictures. These pictures portray a life that doesn't exist. Why? Because they're hiding. They don't want others to know who they really are. Revealing details of their lives hurts too much.

Not everyone goes to that extreme. But each day, you probably see teens hiding who they truly are under a ton of makeup, sexy clothes, or a sarcastic tongue. Some are in youth group every week. But at school, choices are made to be accepted by the crowd. Some of these choices might seem minor. Others have more serious consequences that last a lifetime—for example, choosing to fit in by getting wasted on drugs or alcohol. Or choosing to sleep around to gain popularity. Either choice means taking yourself out of control and giving that control to a substance or to someone else who is willing to use you. Regaining control isn't so easy. And anything can happen when you've temporarily lost control. Sadly, you hear statistics of drunken teens who woke up to the awful discovery that they'd been raped or robbed in some other way.

But fitting in with the crowd isn't the only way we try to hide, is it? When we blow it, we think we can hide from God. But the reality is this: You can run, but you can't truly hide.

The tendency to hide from God when we feel ashamed was inherited from our parents, Adam and Eve. Their story is told in Genesis 2–3 in the Bible.

The choice

From the beginning, God liked hanging out with Adam and Eve. God is a spirit and normally does not have a body, since He is everywhere at once. Yet He must have taken on a body in order to walk and talk with Adam and Eve. They had a standing invitation every day to meet with Him in the garden. There they would walk with Him and enjoy His wonderful presence. This daily garden party would have continued for them and eventually for us, but Adam and Eve stopped going to the party because they were ashamed of what they had done and of what had been done to them.

Eve had believed a lie, and when it came time to meet with God, she wanted to hide from Him instead. You see, the life God had planned for Eve was what we would now call a fairy tale. Her husband adored her and he listened to her every whim and fancy. She was a perfect ten in his eyes. They were in such agreement that they were known by the same name, Mr. and Mrs. Adam. In fact, Eve had been created from a rib from Adam's own body! (See Genesis 2:20–23.) Because they were one with each other, there was no need to identify him independently from her. What she wanted, he wanted.

They had way more than they needed. Every desire they had was satisfied since the land they lived in was filled with gold, pearls, and onyx. Sounds awesome, huh? They lived in the garden called Eden, which means "pleasure and delight," and it was filled with every imaginable fruit for their enjoyment. There were no weeds in their fields or blight on their fruit trees and roses. Best of all, they could hang out with God!

Talk about having it all!

God gave them everything He had created because He loved them. He even told them to eat from the Tree of Life, which gave them immortality. You hear stories of people like Spanish explorer Ponce de León's search for the fountain of youth or myths about potions that grant immortality. But Adam and Eve were faced with the real thing. They could live forever. But there was one tree that God told them not to eat from: the Tree of Knowledge of Good and Evil. Why that tree? Because with that knowledge came the painful understanding of the difference between blessing and calamity (see Genesis 2:15–17). Only this one thing was withheld from them, but even that was because of His great desire to protect them from pain. But Mrs. Adam became curious.

Imagine with me how it might have happened:

> One morning, Mrs. Adam asked, "Why is this Tree of Knowledge of Good and Evil bad for us?"
>
> "I don't know why it's not good for us, but we are to simply trust Him," Mr. Adam explained.
>
> "I don't even understand what it means not to trust Him. Help me to understand, lest I accidentally do the very thing I shouldn't do," she pleaded.
>
> "Just stay away from the tree. To trust God means to obey Him. He has given us unlimited freedom to enjoy all that our eyes can see. The only thing He has asked of us is that we don't eat fruit from that one tree. Once we eat of it, we will understand what evil is. I do know that evil is everything that God is not."
>
> "That's it?" Mrs. Adam responded with surprise. "All that my eyes behold is ours? Everything is ours except that one tree? What more could we possibly want than what we see here in our own home?" So Mrs. Adam was content with all that the Lord had given to her—at least for a while longer.

Life or death, blessings or calamity had been laid before her. The power of choice was hers. She could choose to enjoy all that pleased her loving God, or she could choose to experience everything that He cast away from His presence. She could choose to taste the fruit that nourished her life, or to swallow garbage that would drain the very essence of her life.

What would you have done?

What if you had been the first female to be tempted to do the wrong thing? How long would you have resisted the fruit of the Tree of Knowledge of Good and Evil? How long would you have lasted in the garden of Eden? Perhaps the more important question for any of us is, *How long did we last before we turned to the dark side—the knowledge of evil?*

It doesn't matter if we were the first female on earth or the one billionth female to face the choice of blessing or calamity. Adam failed the test, and every man who was born after him failed to choose life. Following him, we have all failed the test. We have all used the liberty of our free will to choose curses instead of God's blessing in our lives. Paul, an apostle and writer of letters in the New Testament, recorded our predicament:

> All have sinned and are falling short of the honor and glory which God bestows and receives.
>
> Romans 3:23 AMP

No one is without sin. Yes, Mrs. Adam, the woman who had everything that was good, wanted more. But if all we have had is good, the only thing we haven't had is the experiential grief of having nothing. That is what our enemy, Satan, the devil, wants for all of mankind. He wants to take away our blessings because he knows that the only way he can hurt God is to hurt God's children. He's in a war against God (see Ephesians 6:10–20 on pages 200–201), and the battle is over our souls. His only weapon against us is his ability to deceive us through twisting the truth.

In Adam and Eve's time, Satan appeared to Mrs. Adam in the form of a serpent. His goal was to plant doubt in her heart against her Creator:

> "Isn't it true that God said you could not eat of every tree in the garden?"
>
> "We may eat of all the trees except the one called the Knowledge of Good and Evil. We aren't to touch that one or we will

die." But God had not told them not to *touch* it. He told them not to *eat* of it.

Satan used her own misunderstanding against her. "You won't die," he said confidently, knowing that touching it would not destroy her, but that eating it would. He continued, "Go ahead, touch it and see if what I say is true. Not only that," he added, "if you eat of it, you will be like God, who knows the difference between good and evil."

So Mrs. Adam touched the fruit that had tempted her and discovered that she did not die. She then doubted the instruction the Lord had given her. Holding the fruit in her hand, she examined this forbidden mystery. She concluded it would be good to be like God, whose friendship she enjoyed each evening. So she took the fruit to Mr. Adam, and they explored together the one thing God said they should not have.

Some philosophers defend Eve's fall into sin as a sincere drive to know God better. The Bible mentions clearly that she was *deceived* by Satan. Perhaps she believed she would think more like the Father they loved if she knew the difference between good and evil.

God's Word does not say that Adam was deceived. It says that he heeded the voice of his wife, implying that with full knowledge of the consequences, he made a decision to do something against God's instruction. He listened to her and knowingly chose disobedience to God in order to be with her.

Can you see the great war that the enemy has waged over the woman? He could not have worked through the woman in this way unless a high value had been placed on her by her husband and God. The serpent/Satan knew the influence she had over her husband. But he did not foresee the great lengths to which God would go to win her back.

As the bitterness of the fruit dripped onto their lips, Adam and Eve were filled with panic. In that millisecond of deception and disobedience they instantly knew the horror of regret, the despair of remorse, and the loneliness of feeling separated from all the goodness of God. That one act of tasting forbidden fruit caused them to be suddenly alienated from one another, though moments before they had known each other so well.

They wanted to hide, and so they did.

Why are you hiding?

Ever play Hide and Seek when you were a kid? Some kids were probably better than others at hiding. Maybe you were pretty good at it. But *everyone* is bad at it when it comes to God. Hiding from a God who is everywhere is impossible! He will always find you, no matter where you hide.

After Adam and Eve had eaten the fruit of the tree that God had told them to resist, they heard God walking in the garden and hid in the trees. It was time for the party, but the guests of honor refused to come.

God called to Adam, which is what He called both of them in those days, and He said, "Where are you?" But they would not answer Him.

Have you ever been shopping in a department store and heard the code for a lost child announced? Maybe you recall a time when you were a kid and were lost. Some kids like to hide from their parents. They crawl under racks of clothing, giggling to themselves, not knowing the panic they're causing. There is nothing more heartrending than seeing a mother who cannot find her child in a large public place. She knows the possibilities are endless as to where her child may have gone.

An unbearable grief instantly grips the mother's heart as she considers that something may have happened that will keep her from ever seeing her child again. She calls with compassion and panic, "Where are you? Please come to me from wherever you are!" Everyone in the store rallies to help her find the lost child and restore her to her loving mother. And everyone cheers when the child is once again in her mother's arms.

God cried out to Adam and Eve with the same compassion that a mother has for her lost child. Yes, He knew where they were, and He knew that they had done something that would make them want to keep hiding from Him for the rest of their lives. That must have grieved Him more than we can comprehend. He knew that if Adam and Eve couldn't stand before Him without shame, they would never enjoy the true delight of His love that He intended for them to receive.

Please follow my paraphrased version of Genesis 3:8–24, recalling the painful conversation they had, and consider if this is a conversation that you might have had with God if you had done the one thing He had told you not to do.

God called out to His children, "Where are you, Adam?"
Adam responded, "I am afraid of You because I am ashamed."
God asked him, "Who told you to be ashamed?"
But Adam dropped his eyes and looked away from his Father.
"Have you done the one thing I commanded you not to do?" God asked him, hoping that Adam would admit his mistake.
But Adam couldn't confess the truth, so he said, "The woman You gave to me gave me the fruit that I ate."
And Eve couldn't confess her mistake, for she said, "The serpent tricked me into eating the fruit."

I wonder what would have happened if they had admitted their wrongdoing. What if they had confessed their secret sin? Would the horrid consequences of their wrongdoing have been changed?

God knew that if they could see how much He loved them, they would not be afraid to tell Him the truth, so He initiated

My Story

In middle school I was so ecstatic about saving my virginity for marriage—I even got my promise ring along with my friends. But once I got to high school, boys were cuter than ever, my hormones were raging, and I broke my promise. My "hubbie" at the time was really close to my family, and no one could tell me that I wasn't in love or that we wouldn't get married in the future, so I thought it was okay for us to just "do it."

I felt so ashamed and disappointed in my choice that it was hard for me to admit to my mom, even though she suspected something was "different" about me. She asked me about it one day, and although I was so scared of her reaction, I told her the truth. I felt so much better about myself in the end, knowing that my mom still loved me despite my decisions that detoured from her direction.

Too often we are enslaved by our secrets, carrying the burdens of fear, worry, and doubt about our truth and unable to grow. However, I believe it is the will of my Father to walk in the light of my truth, no matter how unpleasant or unpleasing it may seem. As a princess of God, I will remain open, strong, and courageous enough to tell the truth and accept the truths of others. I refuse to pretend that God is not omniscient or that I am not loved and accepted *no matter what* secrets I've had.

Kimari

His great plan of redemptive love for Adam, for Eve, and for us all. One day, He would send a Savior who would seek out those who were lost. (For more on salvation, see page 185.)

Tough love

After telling Adam and Eve of the consequences their choice to do evil would bring into their lives, God demonstrated His love for them by making garments to cover their nakedness so they would come out of their hiding places. He covered their shame with the skins of an animal, thus illustrating the first death and sacrifice of life to pay for the wages of sin. This was a foreshadowing of Jesus' death, the final Lamb who was sacrificed for our sins.

Knowing that underneath their new clothes, they still felt ashamed of themselves, God sent them away from the Tree of Life, to prevent them from eating it and living forever in their broken relationship with Him (see Genesis 3:22–23). God put them out of Eden because He loved them. It is difficult to comprehend, but keeping them from the Tree of Life was an act of grace—of tough love. He didn't want them to live forever with this guilt and shame on them. He separated them from the Tree of Life and immediately began His plan to win His children back.

Have you experienced tough love? Maybe a parent has threatened to kick you or a sibling out if you don't abide by the rules. Or maybe you've been grounded for breaking a rule. Resentment threatens to kick in when your freedom is threatened. "I'm doing this for your own good" falls on deaf ears.

But you can choose to submit to discipline instead of resenting it. You can choose to see the *love* instead of only the *tough*.

Who told you to be ashamed?

God wasn't the one who told Adam and Eve to be ashamed. He didn't suddenly uninvite them to the garden party. He faithfully waited for them. The invitation was still standing, even though He knew what they had done. It was their loss of innocence, their failure to trust Him, and their knowledge of evil that robbed them of their confidence to approach Him. Their secret sin— their rebellion against His instructions—had caused them to be ashamed of themselves. He wanted to restore them to the place where they would run with open arms to Him again.

It didn't matter to God who was first to sin. The one who was seduced and the one who knowingly submitted to seduction both suffered the shame of a secret that they didn't want to confess before God. Adam and Eve were both ashamed.

It doesn't matter to God if you were the offender or the victim—the despair of sin is still the same. God doesn't want you to live forever with that sense of shame separating you from His love.

God doesn't care about your secrets; He cares about your freedom to be honest with Him. He invites you to come out of hiding and into His arms, where He can restore the relationship of love and trust that He has always planned for you.

If you have secrets that make you want to hide from God, He wants you to confess those things to Him. He invites you to accept His power to overcome the secrets in your life. He will give you and anyone else His overcoming power to fight off temptation. He invites you to draw near to Him when you feel weak or afraid. When you do, He will fill you with His magnificent strength so you can triumphantly walk away from the pain of your past and begin a new life in Him.

God gives you the power to choose: His love or the compromises you make to fit in with the crowd or to follow your own agenda. Which will you choose?

> I have set before you life and death, blessings and curses. Now choose life.
>
> Deuteronomy 30:19

WHAT'S *your* STORY?

Tempted to hide? Instead of hiding from God, why not let God hide you? Read the verse below. Write a letter to your Secret

Keeper, telling Him all the things that bother you—especially the things that make you want to hide from Him. He offers you a place of safety. What comforts you most about a place of safety?

> For in the day of trouble he will keep me safe in his dwelling; he will hide me in the shelter of his sacred tent and set me high upon a rock.
>
> Psalm 27:5

What difficult choices are you facing this week? In what ways do you need God's help or provision of safety? Journal about that.

CHAPTER 5

Is That Any Way for a Princess to Act?

Life is like a fairy tale. . . .

Well, she'd done it. Ella had clicked Yes to answer the Evite. But after closing out of the Evite on her phone, she noticed the gazes of Olivia and Marilla in her direction. They must have received a message noting Ella's acceptance.

"Don't tell me *you're* invited to the ball," said Marilla. "A nobody like you."

As Ella headed to her room, she heard Olivia say, "She thinks she's all that."

"Girl, don't even make me laugh," said Marilla.

At times like this, Ella felt so low, she could almost do something drastic. She never pretended that she thought she was better or prettier than anyone else. In fact, she never felt uglier in her life.

PLAYLIST

"Beautiful Beyond Description (I Stand in Awe)" performed by Beth Croft (written by Mark Altrogge)

"The Man in the Mirror" performed by Keke Palmer (written by Siedah Garrett and Glen Ballard)

"My Only Hope" performed by Seventh Day Slumber (written by Joseph Rojas)

Who's the fairest?

Many fairy tales are about beautiful princesses in trouble. In the story of Snow White, being beautiful put Snow White in danger. The evil queen wanted to be the most beautiful woman in the kingdom. But the lovely princess Snow White, who did not desire to be counted as the fairest one in all the land, was given the honor because of her pure heart and gentle ways.

The evil queen kept looking in her magic mirror, asking who was the fairest in the land. A princess doesn't need to go to the mirror and ask, "Who's the fairest of us all?" She understands that her worth is defended by all the soldiers in her father's kingdom. She doesn't need to feel like she is the most beautiful or the most talented in all the land. She knows her value is not based on her performance but on who her father is. Her value is inherited and is unconditional. Although she can change what she does, nothing can change who she is—the precious daughter of the King.

A princess also doesn't have to pretend to be greater than those who defend her. The wisest princess humbly uses her protected freedom to serve others who are less fortunate than she. Beautiful is the princess whose eyes are on the needs of her subjects and not upon herself.

Speaking of beauty, we're surrounded by images that are meant to reflect the ideal of beauty. Cover models peer at us from magazines. Internet pages flash photos of toned celebrities at the beach or on the runway. According to the old saying, "Beauty is in the eye of the beholder." But what's your take on the subject? Take this survey to see!

Beauty is . . .

For each question, circle the answer(s) that best fits your view.

1. Which of the following descriptions fits the image of beauty you *see* every day? (This is what people at your school or in your neighborhood would define as beautiful.)

   a. A tall, thin supermodel type with fair skin and long, luxuriant hair.

   b. A tall, thin supermodel type of any race with long, luxuriant hair.

   c. A tall, thin model with an afro and an attitude.

   d. Athletic, well-toned abs.

   e. Multiple piercings and tattoos.

   f. Pixie haircut; preppy style.

   g. Ethnic pride (in hairstyle, clothes, the works).

   h. Confidence regardless of race.

   i. Other: _____.

2. Which of the following statements fits *your* image of beauty?

   a. A tall, thin supermodel type with fair skin and long, luxuriant hair.

   b. A tall, thin supermodel type of any race with long, luxuriant hair.

   c. A plus-size model radiating confidence.

   d. Athletic, well-toned abs.

   e. Short hair well styled; healthy skin.

    f. Multiple piercings and tattoos.

    g. The image I see in the mirror—me!

    h. A combination of the answers above, namely _____ , _____ , _____.

    i. Other: _____.

3. What do you think a girl needs to feel beautiful?

    a. Great hair.

    b. A trim waistline.

    c. The right cleansers and cosmetics.

    d. Having a killer body (the perfect-sized breasts, toned thighs and arms).

    e. To have inner strength.

    f. None of the above.

    g. A, B, and C.

    h. Only A and B.

4. What's more important to you?

    a. To be beautiful inside.

    b. To be beautiful outside.

    c. To get good grades.

    d. All of the above.

    e. Only A and B.

5. What would you do to be beautiful if you could afford it?

    a. Hit the spa every week.

    b. Have my teeth fixed (dental implants, whitening, the works).

    c. Get breast implants.

    d. Have gastric bypass surgery.

    e. Get permanent eyeliner.

    f. Get a tattoo or another piercing.

    g. Other: _____.

6. How much time do you spend on maintenance (washing
your hair, doing your makeup, getting manicures, etc.)?
   a. Half an hour or less a day.
   b. 1–2 hours a day.
   c. 3–4 hours a day.
   d. 2 hours a week.
   e. Who has time to be beautiful?
   f. Other: _____.

Dove featured a video that showed how people view their own
beauty (see Resources on page 197). Forensic artist Gil Zamora
sketched various women based on their own descriptions of
themselves. They tended to see themselves as less attractive than
they really were. What would you have said if he'd asked you to
describe yourself? Dove ended the video with the tagline: "You
are more beautiful than you think." But many people have a
hard time believing that. Are you one of them? While you think
about that, let me tell you about another young woman—Esther.
Her life was like a fairy tale. You can find that story in the Bible.

A biblical fairy tale

It all started when Vashti, the wife of a king named Xerxes,
angered her husband to the point where he decided to look for
a new queen. Check out Esther 1 for that part of the story. In
chapter 2, we meet Esther:

> Later when King Xerxes' fury had subsided, he remembered
> Vashti and what she had done and what he had decreed about
> her. Then the king's personal attendants proposed, "Let a search
> be made for beautiful young virgins for the king. "Let the king
> appoint commissioners in every province of his realm to bring
> all these beautiful women into the harem at the citadel of Susa.

Let them be placed under the care of Hegai, the king's eunuch, who is in charge of the women; and let beauty treatments be given to them. Then let the young woman who pleases the king be queen instead of Vashti." This advice appealed to the king, and he followed it.

Now there was in the citadel of Susa a Jew of the tribe of Benjamin, named Mordecai son of Jair, the son of Shimei, the son of Kish, who had been carried into exile from Jerusalem by Nebuchadnezzar king of Babylon, among those taken captive with Jehoiachin king of Judah. Mordecai had a cousin named Hadassah, whom he had brought up because she had neither father nor mother. This young woman, who was also known as Esther, had a lovely figure and was beautiful. Mordecai had taken her as his own daughter when her father and mother died.

When the king's order and edict had been proclaimed, many young women were brought to the citadel of Susa and put under the care of Hegai. Esther also was taken to the king's palace and entrusted to Hegai, who had charge of the harem. She pleased him and won his favor. Immediately he provided her with her beauty treatments and special food. He assigned to her seven female attendants selected from the king's palace and moved her and her attendants into the best place in the harem.

Esther 2:1–9

When you read a story like that, how do you feel? Would you have wanted to be Esther? What part of her story appeals to you most?

Although God isn't mentioned, He put Esther in the right place at the right time for a very good reason: to save her people from extermination (see Esther 3–4). So this wasn't about beauty—though Esther was beautiful—but about necessity. But most of us, if we're honest, wonder if we'd make it past the first stage of the beauty pageant. We wonder if we would have been chosen as queen based on how we look.

What you see every day can have a direct effect on how you see yourself. Let's talk more about the mirrors that make up many teens' view of beauty.

Are you looking into mirrors or out of windows?

Your bathroom mirror isn't the only mirror you look at each day. For many teens, the Internet, TV shows, fashion magazines, and peer pressure are the "mirrors" they view every day. These "mirrors" reflect back the prevailing images of beauty. Many teens dream of being on reality shows like *America's Next Top Model*, where unknown girls learn to be runway models. Not only that, televised beauty pageants highlight the faces of beauty. But the standards of beauty are in a constant state of flux. Don't believe it? Take a look at magazine covers or photos of models or movie stars over the last sixty years, and you can see the changes. Models and actresses are getting thinner and thinner.

Media coverage—that includes social media—has a huge effect on how preteens and teens view their bodies. The search for beauty has caused some teens to get breast implants, go on drastic diets, and do other things to fit the standard of beauty. In chapter 2, I talked about how negative body images are shown through eating disorders. An article by Caroline Knorr talks about the pressures female teens face in our looks-conscious society:

> Whether on YouTube or Facebook, girls now feel more pressure to be "camera-ready"—as if to say that the only way to be valued is to appear sexy.
>
> And all this pressure to live up to such narrow beauty standards has contributed to a growing number of online communities dedicated to promoting unhealthy behavior.[1]

Starving oneself is one of those unhealthy ways. But there are others equally as harmful. For some teens, it's not about beauty, but about control . . . or the lack of it in their lives.

A broken mirror

Another "mirror" teens face is the pressure to succeed. Many schools emphasize test scores as the mirror by which your success is measured. School itself can be a pressure cooker, with grades, homework demands, and extracurricular activities. Added to the stress is the desire some have to be popular—another way of "succeeding." Still others aren't as concerned with success as they are with survival. They simply want the nightmare of being bullied to end.

With so much pressure, some teens try to release the pressure any way they can—even self-injuring ways (cutting, burning the skin, sticking objects into one's skin). Some claim they feel a sense of "relief" rather than pain. According to S.A.F.E. (Self Abuse Finally Ends):

> Self-injury is an attempt to cope with a problem and not the problem itself. It is often a cry for help (either conscious or unconscious). Most self-injurers experience themselves as being invisible. Ignoring the behavior only validates this belief, possibly causing them to become even more dangerous to themselves. The key is to focus on the underlying feelings and issues rather than focusing on the behavior itself.[2]

Can you see yourself or someone you know in this mirror? Perhaps the emotional pain is so great, you don't see any way out. But there is. It takes courage and hard work to get the help desperately needed. See page 195 if you or someone you know wants answers or help.

My Story

During my fourth- through seventh-grade years, I dealt with low self-esteem. No matter what my family said, how much they showered me with love, I never thought I was good enough, small enough, or pretty enough. The opinion of others was a tremendous weight and was becoming too much to carry!

At the beginning of eighth grade, I had an epiphany. The Scripture my parents had been telling me was true—"as he thinks in his heart, so is he" (NKJV). I started to really look at the girls I thought had such high self-esteem and realized that what they really possessed was arrogance that masked their low self-esteem! I had been envying the very thing that I was! I immediately changed my whole way of thinking. I began to wake up in the morning saying, "I am beautiful and intelligent, and nothing will ever change that!" At first they were only words, but eventually they became my reality. People began to see the change in me, but more importantly, I saw the change!

Princess, you are fearfully and wonderfully made, and you are *beautiful*! Remember, you are the best you that there will ever be!

Latrice

Mirrors can only reflect. They can't show you a different view. Maybe it's time for a better view. Ever walk by a window only to be stunned by the beautiful view? That's why many people use the phrase *window of opportunity*. It is a positive, hopeful image. I invite you now to take a look out of a window and see a beautiful sight: the Savior.

A window to the Savior

The Old Testament prophet Isaiah wrote a profile of someone who suffered greatly.

He grew up before him like a tender shoot, and like a root out of dry ground. He had no beauty or majesty to attract us

63

to him, nothing in his appearance that we should desire him. He was despised and rejected by mankind, a man of suffering, and familiar with pain. Like one from whom people hide their faces he was despised, and we held him in low esteem.

Surely he took up our pain and bore our suffering, yet we considered him punished by God, stricken by him, and afflicted. But he was pierced for our transgressions, he was crushed for our iniquities; the punishment that brought us peace was on him, and by his wounds we are healed.

Isaiah 53:2–5

This is a profile of the Savior—the One for whom Israel waited for centuries. But the long-promised Savior had not arrived on earth at the time this passage was written. God helped Isaiah understand what the Savior's character and ministry would be like. Isaiah's prophecy would help people recognize the Savior when He arrived.

This Savior is Jesus. But reread the second verse again: "He had no beauty or majesty to attract us to him, nothing in his appearance that we should desire him." Imagine that. Yet we know that Jesus did not look into mirrors and submit to anxiety over His appearance. No, He looked out through the windows of compassion and saw each new day as an opportunity to lift someone, to heal someone, to lead someone back to a closer relationship with God, the Father.

Jesus was mistreated and rejected while on earth—just as the above passage in Isaiah promised. He faced every kind of hurt. He was human like us, but God *unlike* us. He faced the horror of the cross for all of us.

Because of that, He invites you to come to Him with your worst fear or pain. You don't need to wait for an Evite. Here's your invitation right here:

Therefore, since we have a great high priest who has ascended into heaven, Jesus the Son of God, let us hold firmly to the faith we profess. For we do not have a high priest who is unable to empathize with our weaknesses, but we have one who has been tempted in every way, just as we are—yet he did not sin. Let us then approach God's throne of grace with confidence, so that we may receive mercy and find grace to help us in our time of need.

Hebrews 4:14–16

A window to a hurting world

Once we get to know Jesus, He gives us the power to exchange our self-gratifying mirrors for windows that allow us to see the needs of others the way Jesus did. I remember a most significant day when I met a young woman who needed encouragement. I could not have encouraged her if I had never been where she had been, if I had never felt alone or had forgotten the way she was feeling that day. But it is also true that I could not have helped her if I was so busy looking in a mirror, seeing only my reflection.

I realized how far the Lord had brought me by seeing myself in that young woman's eyes. Her need to know Him was great. I was blessed to be the one to introduce her to her heavenly Father, to her inheritance in Him, and to her new title of princess.

Are you game to turn from the mirror and face a hurting world?

Beauty is more than how you look. Beauty is in how you accept others for who they are—like Jesus. It comes from inside no matter what the image in the mirror suggests or what society dictates. And when you accept how beautiful you are inside, you can't help seeing the beauty in others. Are you willing to do whatever you can to help bring out the beauty in others?

Are you Mary, Michal, or the daughter of Herodias?

I believe three kinds of teens are reading this book. You could be like Mary, the mother of Jesus, who as a young woman was open to be used of God to be a blessing to others—to encourage them to see their inner beauty. Or you might be like Michal, a young woman who searched for others to blame for her unhappiness. Or you could be like the daughter of Herodias (unnamed in the Gospels, but identified as Salome), a young woman whose beauty was used by others as a hindrance.

Let's start with Mary. You can find that story in Luke 1:26–38. You've heard the story of the angel Gabriel's visit to Mary. She was probably a young teen at this point—just your average young woman. But she was hit with the news that she was chosen to be the mother of the Savior. Amazing news, considering she was a virgin. Normally, a pregnancy outside of wedlock was an automatic death sentence. Mary's fiancé, Joseph, could have accused her publicly of adultery—a crime punishable by stoning.

What would you have said to the angel if you were Mary? Mary gave this beautiful reply:

> "I am the Lord's servant," Mary answered. "May your word to me be fulfilled."
>
> Luke 1:38

Could you have responded that way, even with an angel standing before you? Mary knew the beauty of being God's servant. Even though hard days lay ahead, she knew that God could make something beautiful out of her life. And He did. She became the mother to the King of the Universe.

Moving on to Michal, we can find her story in 1 and 2 Samuel. Michal was a princess whose life seemed to be a fairy tale at first. She totally dug David when he was the hero everyone talked about after he killed Goliath (see 1 Samuel 18:20). What's more, she married the handsome hero. Sweet, huh?

When her father, King Saul, grew jealous of David and tried to have David killed, Michal hid David (1 Samuel 19). But later, Saul took Michal away from David and ordered her to marry someone else (1 Samuel 25:44). Later David reclaimed her as his wife. Maybe Michal felt used—passed from man to man. By then, bitterness had built up. When David celebrated the return of the ark to Jerusalem by dancing in the street, we learn how Michal felt. That story can be found in 2 Samuel 6:16–23. Here is part of that passage:

> As the ark of the Lord was entering the city of David, Saul's daughter Michal looked down from the window and saw King David leaping and dancing before the Lord, and she despised him in her heart. . . .
>
> When David returned home to bless his household, Saul's daughter Michal came out to meet him. "How the king of Israel honored himself today!" she said. "He exposed himself today in the sight of the slave girls of his subjects like a vulgar person would expose himself."
>
> 2 Samuel 6:16, 20 HCSB

Michal was a princess with a king-sized temper. Lashing out at David in bitterness cost Michal dearly. She was never able to have a child after that.

Is Michal's example too bitter for you? Let's move on to another princess—Salome, the daughter of Herodias. She wasn't bitter; she was actually obedient—to her selfish mother. You can find that story in Matthew 14:1–12. Her mother, Herodias, had left her husband (Herod Philip) and married another man—King Herod Antipas. When John the Baptist, the great prophet and relative of Jesus, called her out on that (this marriage wasn't considered legal), Herodias decided to use her young daughter to get revenge against John. At a party thrown by Herod, the daughter of Herodias performed a sexy dance. Because he was so thrilled with the dance, Herod vowed to give her whatever she wanted. And what would a girl want? Diamonds? Nope!

> So she, having been prompted by her mother, said, "Give me John the Baptist's head here on a platter."
>
> Matthew 14:8 NKJV

You have a choice: to be like Mary—obedient to God; to be like Michal—obedient to your own desires; or to be like the daughter of Herodias—obedient to the wrong person. Which will you choose?

WHAT'S *your* STORY?

Reread the following verses from Isaiah 53. Jesus bore your wrongs and your pain on the cross. He knows what it's like to be hurt and rejected. Write a note to God and tell Him your pain, your anger, and your fear. Exchange the things that bother you with the peace He offers. If you don't feel like writing a paragraph, draw a picture or jot down a few words that describe how you feel.

> Surely he took up our pain and bore our suffering, yet we considered him punished by God, stricken by him, and afflicted. But he was pierced for our transgressions, he was crushed for our iniquities; the punishment that brought us peace was on him, and by his wounds we are healed.
>
> Isaiah 53:4–5

Consider the world's standards for beauty. How do you feel about them? How have they helped or harmed you? Be real with God about them in your journal or below.

CHAPTER 6

We Are Family

Life is like a fairy tale. . . .

When her father married her stepmother, Ella hoped she would get the family she'd dreamed about. Having been an only child for so long, she was thrilled to finally have two sisters near her age.

But reality was nothing like the dream. Her stepmother and Olivia and Marilla were an army united against her. Marilla seemed especially spiteful. Thanks to her snippy comments, Ella had begun to think of Marilla as Cruella. And Olivia wasn't much nicer.

What had she done to make them dislike her so much? Other than walk and breathe, Ella couldn't think of anything.

Her father was no help. He always took her stepmother's side, even when she was wrong. "To keep peace," he explained, his eyes weary.

Ella couldn't wait to be eighteen and off to college. Maybe once she left, she'd never return.

PLAYLIST

"We Are Family" performed by Sister Sledge and Jade (written by Bernard Edwards and Nile Rodgers)

"Here for You" performed by Matt Maher and Matt Redman (written by Matt Maher, Matt Redman, Jesse Reeves, Tim Wanstall)

"Mary, Don't You Weep" performed by Yolanda Adams

Can we all get along?

Brothers and sisters—they grow with us and see us at our worst. They know just the right buttons to push, don't they, with their teasing.

Do you have siblings? Answer the following questions by marking where you are on each line below.

1. How well do you get along?

| 1 | 2 | 3 | 4 | 5 | 6 | 7 | 8 | 9 | 10 |

We fight all the time   We get along great

2. How much time do you spend with your siblings?

| 1 | 2 | 3 | 4 | 5 | 6 | 7 | 8 | 9 | 10 |

No time   We hang out all the time

3. How much do you have in common with your brother or sister?

| 1 | 2 | 3 | 4 | 5 | 6 | 7 | 8 | 9 | 10 |

Nothing except blood   We like the same things
and an address

Add siblings and blend

With more and more people remarrying, families are becoming blended and extended. Maybe you're in a blended family like

Ella, having to get along with stepbrothers and stepsisters. Or maybe you're in a foster home and suddenly have foster siblings to get to know. What do you do to get along and maintain peace? Or is peace an issue?

Some blends work well, others don't—like two patterns of stripes matched together. Sometimes people ignore each other to maintain peace. They see silence as a better alternative to fighting. The news is full of stories of family tension. Some homes are war zones with simmering tempers ready to explode. In other homes, family members haven't spoken to other family members in years because of unresolved hurts. Still others snap and harm their family members and others.

Family tension is nothing new. It's been brewing for thousands of years.

Brothers and sisters in the Bible

The Bible is full of stories of siblings, most involving brothers: Cain and Abel (Genesis 4); Isaac and Ishmael (Genesis 21); Jacob and Esau (Genesis 25:21–34; 27–28; 32–33); Joseph and his eleven brothers (Genesis 37–50; they also had a sister, Dinah); Moses and Aaron (most of Exodus, Leviticus, Numbers, and the first part of Deuteronomy; they had a sister, Miriam); David and his seven brothers (1 Samuel 16–17); Peter and Andrew (John 1:40–42); James and John (Mark 10:35–45); and many others. In many cases, the father's sins caused family strife that lasted for generations. For example, because of David's sin with Bathsheba (2 Samuel 11), family feuds escalated. Soon his sons were killing each other (2 Samuel 13). We see a lot of that in our time.

Even Jesus was not exempt from family trouble, though He was the responsible older brother. You see, His brothers and sisters— the sons and daughters of Joseph and Mary—didn't believe He was the promised Savior. Like most siblings, they gave Him a hard time. Think how you would react if *your* brother announced that He was the Savior prophets spoke about for hundreds of years.

The gospel of John has the story of a tense family moment in Jesus' life.

> After this, Jesus went around in Galilee. He did not want to go about in Judea because the Jewish leaders there were looking for a way to kill him. But when the Jewish Festival of Tabernacles was near, Jesus' brothers said to him, "Leave Galilee and go to Judea, so that your disciples there may see the works you do. No one who wants to become a public figure acts in secret. Since you are doing these things, show yourself to the world." For even his own brothers did not believe in him.
>
> John 7:1–5

But Jesus' family drama has a happy ending. At least two of His brothers, James and Jude, changed their tune about Jesus. After becoming faith-filled Christians, they also became church leaders and wrote letters that became part of the New Testament.

Knowing what family drama was like was the reason Jesus could tell such convincing stories about families. One of the most well known is the parable of the lost son (Luke 15:11–32). Though the lost son returned to his family, he had to deal with an angry brother.

With all of this talk of brothers, you might be wondering about sisters. The Bible has stories of sisters too. As with many situations today, the Bible doesn't sugarcoat the conflict between sisters.

Sad sisters

Rachel and Leah were sisters married to the same man—Jacob. You can find that story in Genesis 29–30. Back then, a man could be married to more than one woman. Though Jacob loved Rachel and agreed to work for Laban (father of Rachel and Leah) for seven years in order to marry Rachel, Laban tricked Jacob into marrying Leah. But Laban agreed to let Jacob also marry Rachel if Jacob worked for him another seven years.

Sounds like a bad reality TV show, doesn't it? Imagine being second best in that relationship. Leah, however, could readily do what Rachel could not: have a child. So the rivalry between them continued with Rachel offering her servant to her own husband to gain a child that way. When Leah stopped having children, she did the same. But God made something good come out of that sad situation. Between Leah, Rachel, and their two servants, twelve sons were born to Jacob. Through these sons came the twelve tribes of Israel. In fact, Jacob's name was changed to Israel, because he was the father of this nation (Genesis 32:28).

When Jesus walked the earth, He had three good friends who were in the same family: Mary, Martha, and Lazarus. Jesus often hung out at their house. But Mary and Martha had their differences:

> While they were traveling, He entered a village, and a woman named Martha welcomed Him into her home. She had a sister named Mary, who also sat at the Lord's feet and was listening to what He said. But Martha was distracted by her many tasks, and she came up and asked, "Lord, don't You care that my sister has left me to serve alone? So tell her to give me a hand."
>
> The Lord answered her, "Martha, Martha, you are worried and upset about many things, but one thing is necessary. Mary has made the right choice, and it will not be taken away from her."
>
> Luke 10:38–42 HCSB

How would you have reacted if you were Martha? Maybe you've said similar words because the lion's share of the workload around the house has fallen to you. Learning how to disagree is a lesson you learn when you live with others.

But there is another family to consider, even if your relationships at home are golden.

Other siblings

When you trust Jesus as your Savior, you receive a new family—God's family. That means other Christians are your brothers and sisters. That makes the church the ultimate blended family! (See page 185 for more information on salvation.) In fact, Jesus mentions just that:

> While Jesus was still talking to the crowd, his mother and brothers stood outside, wanting to speak to him. Someone told him, "Your mother and brothers are standing outside, wanting to speak to you."
>
> He replied to him, "Who is my mother, and who are my brothers?" Pointing to his disciples, he said, "Here are my mother and my brothers. For whoever does the will of my Father in heaven is my brother and sister and mother."
>
> Matthew 12:46–50

Jesus is the glue that keeps believers together. This is why the church also is known as the body of Christ. He makes us united.

> Just as a body, though one, has many parts, but all its many parts form one body, so it is with Christ. For we were all baptized by one Spirit so as to form one body—whether Jews or Gentiles, slave or free—and we were all given the one Spirit to drink. Even so the body is not made up of one part but of many.
>
> 1 Corinthians 12:12–14

My Story

I have a younger brother, Braxton. I am five years older than him. While I'm sixteen years old and Braxton is eleven, it doesn't seem like much of an age difference between us now. We have some similar interests (music genres as well as sports). The five-year age difference was more distinct when I was five years old and Braxton was only a newborn. Back then, I didn't know the meaning of the age difference.

There were instances when I felt that, as the older sibling, I had experienced some sort of injustice because Braxton seemed to always get the benefit of the doubt as the younger sibling. This always happened when Braxton never listened to me or followed my advice, utterly upsetting me.

After a while I got over these feelings of selfishness and realized that God placed me in Braxton's life to give him some direction, not utter control. Being the older sibling meant being the bigger person in a lot of situations. God helped me see that, like it or not, I was Braxton's role model. After accepting that, I now try my best to be the best sister for Braxton. This means that I am responsible for having high expectations for both Braxton and myself.

Kennedy

How good and pleasant it is when God's people live together in unity!

Psalm 133:1

But believers sometimes have a hard time getting along. Take a look at 2 Corinthians 2 and Philippians 4 if you need convincing. But you don't need me to prove that Christians don't always get along. There have been stories in the news of church splits and fallouts among Christians for decades.

How do you settle differences with others? Do you fuss and argue? Play the blame game?

God has help for families—biological, spiritual, extended, or otherwise. Think of it as a recipe with several ingredients, all beginning with *F*. The first is *fruit*.

Fruit of the Spirit

The Holy Spirit provides fruit—characteristics that help us get along with each other.

> But the fruit of the Spirit is love, joy, peace, forbearance, kindness, goodness, faithfulness, gentleness and self-control. Against such things there is no law.
>
> Galatians 5:22–23

Love is the first characteristic—the foundation of any relationship. Without love, you can't get along with anyone for very long. Since God is love (1 John 4:8), which means He is the source of love, the Holy Spirit is in charge of growing that and other characteristics in you. All work together. But we can intentionally pursue characteristics like peace by the way we act toward each other, as this verse suggests:

> Keep your tongue from evil and your lips from telling lies. Turn from evil and do good; seek peace and pursue it.
>
> Psalm 34:13–14

The next, but not the least, is *forgiveness*.

Forgiveness

Forgiveness is the willingness to put aside grudges and not hold a wrong against another. It excites me to imagine a church full of people who make it a habit to forgive others. How would the habit of forgiveness change us? How would it change our world?

Children would see the principle of unconditional love demonstrated from their parents. Husbands and wives would enjoy the security of knowing that no matter what happens, there is someone at home who will lift them up when others have cast them down. Employees would face each new day with enthusiasm, having already forgotten the offenses of the day before. It would be like having God's will on earth as it is in heaven. I'll talk more about forgiveness in chapter 9.

Forgiveness is the requirement for our being forgiven by God for our wrongs. I'm not talking about the sin in which we all were born. I'm talking about the times that we offend God on a day-to-day basis. If we refuse to forgive someone, we place a barrier between God's forgiveness and us.

> For if you forgive other people when they sin against you, your heavenly Father will also forgive you. But if you do not forgive others their sins, your Father will not forgive your sins.
>
> Matthew 6:14–15

Jesus also told a story about an unforgiving servant to illustrate this—Matthew 18:21–35. God wants us to knock down any barriers that stand between us and forgiveness.

Yet there are some awful situations that have left us in unimaginable pain. We can't pretend that we have *any* forgiveness within us. At times like that, God still wants us to be honest and admit we're having a hard time.

It's like the story of Corrie ten Boom, a Dutch believer who wrote the book *The Hiding Place*. Because her family helped hide Jewish citizens during World War II, she was placed in a concentration camp after the Gestapo raided their house. Her sister Betsie died in the camp. When Corrie later came face-to-face with one of the guards from that concentration camp, a guard who had become a believer and wanted to shake her hand, she had a hard time extending her hand. God had to help her.[1]

In order to grow, you need to have the next ingredient: *foundation/faith*.

Foundation/Faith

You've seen a new building built, right? Houses and other buildings are built on a foundation. Otherwise, they would sink into the ground. Think also of the building block game Jenga or Legos. If you try to build a tower with a weak foundation, it will quickly fall over.

The Christian faith is built on a foundation too. That foundation is faith in Jesus. Jesus also told a story about having the right foundation:

> Therefore everyone who hears these words of mine and puts them into practice is like a wise man who built his house on the rock. The rain came down, the streams rose, and the winds blew and beat against that house; yet it did not fall, because it had its foundation on the rock. But everyone who hears these words of mine and does not put them into practice is like a foolish man who built his house on sand. The rain came down, the streams rose, and the winds blew and beat against that house, and it fell with a great crash.
>
> Matthew 7:24–27

But that story was more than just a story about having the right building materials. It's really about faith. Some arguments start because of disagreements about faith. Make sure you have the right foundation: belief in Jesus—His death and resurrection. (See also page 185 for more information on salvation.)

This is the heart of the gospel message. Paul, who wrote most of the books in the New Testament, explains the good news in two different New Testament letters:

> What I received I passed on to you as of first importance: that Christ died for our sins according to the Scriptures, that he was buried, that he was raised on the third day according to the Scriptures.
>
> 1 Corinthians 15:3–4

> Consequently, you are no longer foreigners and strangers, but fellow citizens with God's people and also members of his household, built on the foundation of the apostles and prophets, with Christ Jesus himself as the chief cornerstone. In him the whole building is joined together and rises to become a holy temple in the Lord.
>
> Ephesians 2:19–21

Faith is something you can't do without. Next is something else you can't do without: *focus.*

Focus

You know when you really pay attention to something. Think about an eye exam. The doctor tells you to focus on a line of type. All you see is the chart and those letters. You're not looking elsewhere.

We usually focus on that which interests us. For example, that cute guy in biology, or a movie you're really enjoying. God wants you to focus on His Son just as hard.

> If then you have been raised with Christ [to a new life, thus sharing His resurrection from the dead], aim at and seek the [rich, eternal treasures] that are above, where Christ is, seated at the right hand of God.

And set your minds and keep them set on what is above (the higher things), not on the things that are on the earth.

Colossians 3:1–2 AMP

You keep him in perfect peace whose mind is stayed on you, because he trusts in you.

Isaiah 26:3 ESV

If you play a sport involving a ball, you know the first rule is to keep your eye on the ball. That's when you score points. When your keep your eyes on God, all you see is Him. You can focus on Him through prayer and reading God's Word.

When we focus on Jesus, really think about Him, we won't have room in our thoughts for worry or negative emotions like hate. Focusing on Him keeps us out of trouble.

Next is something you can't do alone: *fellowship*.

Fellowship

In New Testament times, new Christians made time to be with others. Check it out:

They devoted themselves to the apostles' teaching and to fellowship, to the breaking of bread and to prayer.

Acts 2:42

They made being together a priority—an important habit. What habits do you have? Hanging out with your friends? Your man? You can make being with other Christians a priority. For example, you could invite someone new to youth group. You can call someone and encourage that person or ask a friend to pray with you. When you meet with other believers, Jesus is right there with you!

Where two or three gather in my name, there am I with them.

Matthew 18:20

Next is the ultimate: *Father*.

Father

If you trust Jesus as your Savior, you don't have to go it alone. You have a heavenly Father who loves you. He is a Father to all who put their faith in Jesus. You're invited to go to Him in prayer anytime.

See what great love the Father has lavished on us, that we should be called children of God! And that is what we are! The reason the world does not know us is that it did not know him.

1 John 3:1

When Jesus taught His disciples to pray, He reminded them that God was the Father. That makes Jesus your Savior *and* your brother. ☺

Our Father in heaven, hallowed be your name. Your kingdom come, your will be done, on earth as it is in heaven. Give us this day our daily bread, and forgive us our debts, as we also have forgiven our debtors. And lead us not into temptation, but deliver us from evil.

Matthew 6:9–13 ESV

God is for you, not against you. He can help you with both families: the one in your home and the one at church. He waits for you to ask for help. You can also pray for both families.

WHAT'S *your* STORY?

Write a letter to your Secret Keeper. Read the following verse. How can this advice help you live in harmony with others? You might write or speak a prayer, asking God for His help.

Live in harmony with one another; do not be haughty (snobbish, high-minded, exclusive), but readily adjust yourself to [people, things] and give yourselves to humble tasks. Never overestimate yourself or be wise in your own conceits.

Romans 12:16 AMP

Has a brother or sister made you angry recently? If so, are you having a hard time forgiving? Talk to God about it.

CHAPTER 7

A Word of Truth

Life is like a fairy tale. . . .

Ella helped her stepsisters and stepmother get ready for the ball, wishing she didn't have to hear them run their mouths.

"Too bad you'll miss the party of the century," all three said over and over.

"But I said I'd go," Ella said softly, as she finished pinning Olivia's hair in an upsweep.

"You?" Marilla scoffed, making herself comfortable on Ella's bed. "Wearing what? You don't have anything decent to wear. I've seen the clothes in your closet. Tacky."

Ella said nothing. She knew very well the lack of nice clothes in her closet. Marilla was right. Who was she kidding?

"Ella, do yourself a favor and stay home," Olivia said, patting Ella's arm. "You're not that good at styling your own hair. I'm only saying it for your own good. You'll only embarrass yourself. The prince will take one look and laugh at you."

Ella sighed. Maybe staying home was a good idea.

PLAYLIST

"Open the Eyes of My Heart" written by Paul Baloche

"To Me" written and performed by Matthew West

"Free" written and performed by Dara Maclean

Hurtful words

Ella's stepsisters thought they were doing Ella a favor by telling her the "truth" about herself. You can imagine how she felt. Has anyone ever shared "truth" like that with you? How did it make you feel?

Many children know the old rhyme, "Sticks and stones may break my bones, but words will never hurt me." Maybe you've said that in the past. But the truth is, words *can* hurt. Words can cause emotional damage that lasts for many years.

That's one reason Jesus said, "You will know the truth, and the truth will set you free"—words recorded in John 8:32. Jesus means more than the truth spoken about in the truth campaign you've seen about tobacco companies. He means Truth with a capital T.

What is truth?

Jesus answered, "You say that I am a king. In fact, the reason I was born and came into the world is to testify to the truth. Everyone on the side of truth listens to me."

"What is truth?" retorted Pilate.

John 18:37–38

Pilate, the Roman governor of Palestine, was confronted by truth during the trial of Jesus. Like Pilate, some people today either aren't sure or flat-out don't believe that absolutes like truth exist. They think that everyone has his or her own version of truth. Has anyone ever said that to you, that truth is relative?

Think of it this way: What if I decided to come up with my own way of measuring things? I could decide that an inch is equal to the size of my thumb. And you could decide that an inch is equal to the tip of your index finger to the second joint.

My Story

For years I searched for acceptance, trying to find things about myself I thought people would love so they would stick around. Then I was blessed to meet someone who allowed me to be myself. We did everything together! We shopped, danced, sang, talked about boys—and most importantly, we ministered together. She knew my deepest secrets.

When I began to feel our friendship shifting, I would cancel my plans so that we could spend time together—but I couldn't find the source of the problem. My heart will never forget the night she ended our friendship. I still have the text messages in my phone. She wrote, "I have always felt this friendship has always been about you. I'd rather be solo."

Where was this coming from? How long had she felt this way? I had been there for her—during her first crush, when she was nervous about going to high school, her very first volleyball game, her baptism. Now I felt alone. I was hurt to the point where I never wanted a best friend again.

But I soon realized the importance of seasonal relationships. Sometimes we give so much to people who are supposed to leave. Yes, I was hurt, but I had to understand that as I grew in God, He was getting ready to take me places she couldn't go. As bad as it may have hurt, I do believe we became better individuals because of our separation.

Briannon

So if I told you a book was six inches by nine inches, that length wouldn't be the same length as it is for you, would it? Think of how chaotic measurements would be if we all used our own standard of measurement.

Just as there is a standard for measuring an inch, there is a standard for truth. Jesus said, "I am the way and the truth and the life. No one comes to the Father except through me"—words from John 14:6. Sounds like He's declaring that there is a truth and *He* is it! That is another reason why Jesus could say, "You will know the truth, and the truth will set you free." As the Truth, He came to die for the sins of all—to set everyone free.

Sometimes the first truth we need to accept is that about ourselves—the fact that we're not perfect. We easily make mistakes. But sometimes when we tell someone the "truth" about himself or herself, we want to be "right" and him or her to be "wrong." This means we have an agenda beyond sharing truth.

A servant of truth

Sometimes people use their words like a weapon. "Truth hurts," they may declare. Perhaps you've been the victim of someone's harsh words like Ella was. They feel it is their duty to tell you the truth about yourself. But they lack love. They're serving their own desires rather than God's.

God never meant for us to wield our words like a blade against each other. Instead, we're to build each other up, as 1 Thessalonians 5:11 suggests: "Therefore encourage one another and build each other up, just as in fact you are doing."

A princess cares for the feelings of her subjects—from those with the highest place in society to the lowest. Though a princess, she is a servant of truth with her words. She doesn't let her rank or pride keep her from being gentle. Why? Because she is assured of the love of her father, the king. She also is assured of her place in the kingdom—at its very center.

You are a princess—the daughter of the King of the Universe. The King loves you. How can you share the truth of that love with others?

Here's one way to think of it. If a friend or family member asked you to keep a secret that might be harmful, would you keep it? For example, what if you knew a friend had an addiction to prescription drugs? To save your friend's life, you wouldn't keep silent, would you? Sometimes people can't see what's true about themselves. When that happens, you might need the support of someone else as you confront that person. The Bible provides a way.

> If your brother or sister sins, go and point out their fault, just between the two of you. If they listen to you, you have won them over. But if they will not listen, take one or two others along, so that "every matter may be established by the testimony of two or three witnesses." If they still refuse to listen, tell it to the church; and if they refuse to listen even to the church, treat them as you would a pagan or a tax collector.
>
> Matthew 18:15–17

A servant of truth confronts with truth. But truth spoken without tact or love has the potential to be a weapon. Here's how you can speak truth God's way:

> Instead, speaking the truth in love, we will grow to become in every respect the mature body of him who is the head, that is, Christ.
>
> Ephesians 4:15

Sound easy? It isn't. It means you're willing to lay down your pride and your desire to be right (even if you are). It means speaking when God gives you the okay—when the time is right. God and you are partners in this. But you're the junior partner and He's the senior. That means His word goes. But the Holy Spirit helps you know what to say. That's how you speak the truth in love.

Freeing yourself with truth

How would you describe yourself? When you think of your performance in a sport, playing a musical instrument, or interviewing for a job, do you think in negative or positive terms? *Oh, that was stupid,* or *I'm so dumb.* Ever think either of those? Sometimes we're our own worst enemy and grade ourselves harshly.

Do you know what's really true about yourself? I don't mean height, weight, birthday, etc. I mean, do you know what you're really capable of? Or do you see only limitations? For example, "I can never be as smart as she is," or "I'll fail if I try."

Do you tend to rely on others' assessment of you? You have to know the truth about yourself for yourself. Here's some truth straight from God's Word:

> I can do all things through Christ who strengthens me.
>
> Philippians 4:13 NKJV

Do you believe that? Your life will never be the same once you accept it.

Here are some other verses on truth. You might read a verse every day and think about it throughout the day.

> Guide me in your truth and teach me, for you are God my Savior, and my hope is in you all day long.
>
> Psalm 25:5

The Lord is near to all who call on him, to all who call on him in truth.

Psalm 145:18

But when he, the Spirit of truth, comes, he will guide you into all the truth. He will not speak on his own; he will speak only what he hears, and he will tell you what is yet to come.

John 16:13

Sanctify them by the truth; your word is truth.

John 17:17

While you think about God's Word, pray, asking God for kind and loving ways to share truth with someone. While you're at it, ask Him for the grace to accept what's true about yourself. Ask Him to open your eyes to the different ways He reveals truth to you, no matter where you are: at home, at school, at church, or in your neighborhood.

WHAT'S *your* STORY?

After you read the verse below, write a note to your Secret Keeper in your journal, answering the following questions:

Instead, speaking the truth in love, we will grow to become in every respect the mature body of him who is the head, that is, Christ.

Ephesians 4:15

When has someone ever spoken truth to you in a loving way? Who needs to know the truth? How can you "speak the truth in love" to those who need it?

CHAPTER 8

Wash Off Those Cinders!

Life is like a fairy tale. . . .

Ella could hardly believe it. She had a fairy godmother! And that fairy godmother said, "Of course you'll go to the ball!" Not only that, she promised to hook Ella up with something totally on point to wear to the ball. Sweet! But before she could dress in her absolute best, first, she had to get cleaned up.

"You can't go looking like you rolled in mud," said her fairy godmother.

As Ella showered, she thought about the ball and how she'd look better than she'd ever looked in the new dress. But suddenly ugly thoughts rose to mind. What if the prince found out what she'd done—how far she'd gone with Josh or that bracelet she'd stolen when she was fourteen and never told anyone about?

PLAYLIST

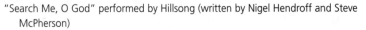

"Search Me, O God" performed by Hillsong (written by Nigel Hendroff and Steve McPherson)

"Create in Me a Clean Heart" written by Keith Green

Getting cleaned up

Ella had lived among the cinders for a long time. She needed to wash those off before dolling up for the night. After all, a dirty face detracts from a gorgeous gown.

Taking care of your body is important. But I'm curious . . .

1. What do you consider a necessary part of your daily cleansing routine?
   a. I'm strictly a soap-and-water girl. Oh, and deodorant.
   b. Acne gel—a necessary evil.
   c. Exfoliating and moisturizing—to keep my skin soft.
   d. Leg shaving or waxing.
   e. All of the above.
   f. Other: _____.

2. Okay, you're clean. Now how much makeup do you use?
   a. Lip gloss or lipstick only.
   b. Eyeliner, eye shadow, blush, foundation, fake eyelashes, nail polish, lipstick—the works.
   c. Lipstick and eye shadow only.
   d. Nail polish and lipstick only.
   e. Eye shadow and lipstick only.
   f. Other: _____.

3. How much money a month do you spend on beauty products?
   a. $10 or less.
   b. $10–$20.
   c. $20–$30.
   d. $30–$50.
   e. $100 and over.
   f. I don't spend money—someone else buys them for me.

The beauty industry is big business—$7 billion a year.[1] Case in point: There is a soap made of 24-karat gold that sells for $24 a bar—ASSO Bar acne soap. But one of the most expensive soaps in the world is Cor Silver Soap, which sells for $120 a bar! A woman will spend, on average, about $15,000 on beauty products throughout her life.[2]

Some people spend more money on skin care products than they can afford. A survey of fifteen- and sixteen-year-olds determined that more money was spent on clothes, beauty products, and accessories than on anything else.[3] How about you?

Washing off cinders isn't just about getting cleaned up on the outside. It also involves getting cleaned up on the inside. That's something God helps you to do. Let me tell you about two women who met Jesus and learned how to get clean inside.

Two women, one Savior

Two women had a need that only Jesus could meet. Here's the story of one:

> A large crowd followed and pressed around him. And a woman was there who had been subject to bleeding for twelve years. She had suffered a great deal under the care of many doctors and had spent all she had, yet instead of getting better she grew worse. When she heard about Jesus, she came up behind him in the crowd and touched his cloak, because she thought, "If I just touch his clothes, I will be healed." Immediately her bleeding stopped and she felt in her body that she was freed from her suffering.
>
> At once Jesus realized that power had gone out from him. He turned around in the crowd and asked, "Who touched my clothes?"
>
> "You see the people crowding against you," his disciples answered, "and yet you can ask, 'Who touched me?'"

My Story

I believe that whether or not certain beauty products are necessary depends on the person. Some people have acne, while other people have different types of blemishes on their skin or uneven pigmentation. And then there are those who just think they need beauty products to be perceived as beautiful. And while some might think that's ridiculous, it really isn't, because I feel that way sometimes too. However, at those times, I try to remind myself that I am fearfully and wonderfully made by God (see Psalm 139:14). God's Word also says that "man looks on the outward appearance, but the Lord looks on the heart" (1 Samuel 16:7).

So when I put my beauty products on, I remind myself that I'm not making myself beautiful but that I am already beautiful because God made me so. And just like me, you will probably need to remind yourself a lot that, even though you see flaws, God sees beauty.

Nia

But Jesus kept looking around to see who had done it. Then the woman, knowing what had happened to her, came and fell at his feet and, trembling with fear, told him the whole truth. He said to her, "Daughter, your faith has healed you. Go in peace and be freed from your suffering."

Mark 5:24–34

Having your period and all that goes with it is never fun, is it? Can you imagine having one for twelve years? In Bible times, when you were on your period, you were considered unclean and not allowed to be in society until it was over. So this woman felt unclean for twelve long years until Jesus healed her. All it took was one touch. Her life was transformed.

That might sound like an extreme story. But what if you substitute *guilt* for *bleeding*? Does that sound less extreme and closer to home? Many people suffer guilt over a hurt or a wrongdoing for many years. They're desperate for God to touch their lives. Like the woman in the next story:

> At dawn [Jesus] appeared again in the temple courts, where all the people gathered around him, and he sat down to teach them. The teachers of the law and the Pharisees brought in a woman caught in adultery. They made her stand before the group and said to Jesus, "Teacher, this woman was caught in the act of adultery. In the Law Moses commanded us to stone such women. Now what do you say?" They were using this question as a trap, in order to have a basis for accusing him.
>
> But Jesus bent down and started to write on the ground with his finger. When they kept on questioning him, he straightened up and said to them, "Let any one of you who is without sin be the first to throw a stone at her." Again he stooped down and wrote on the ground.
>
> At this, those who heard began to go away one at a time, the older ones first, until only Jesus was left, with the woman still standing there. Jesus straightened up and asked her, "Woman, where are they? Has no one condemned you?"
>
> "No one, sir," she said.
>
> "Then neither do I condemn you," Jesus declared. "Go now and leave your life of sin."
>
> John 8:2–11

She'd been caught in the act and faced a death sentence. The crowd around her reminded her of how dirty she was in their eyes. But as she stood there, with the dirt of her wrongs all over her, only one person reached out in grace to her: Jesus. Instead of condemning her, He saved her from an immediate and painful death. More importantly, He had the ability to save her from spiritual death too.

It's easy to judge someone. It's much harder to offer the kind of cleansing someone needs to feel whole inside. That's something only God can do.

Come clean about a dirty habit

Another way to get clean is to come clean about issues beyond your strength to handle—like addictions. The first step for anyone to kick the habit is to admit that there is a problem. Perhaps someone you know might need to come clean. Perhaps that someone is you.

Maybe the addiction is to cigarettes or harder substances like drugs. Maybe it started off with an addiction to a prescription drug that got out of hand.

For some teens, addiction starts with a gateway drug like marijuana or synthetic marijuana (also known as Spice). According to the National Institute on Drug Abuse:

> In 2013, 7.0 percent of 8th graders, 18.0 percent of 10th graders, and 22.7 percent of 12th graders used marijuana in the past month, up from 5.8 percent, 13.8 percent, and 19.4 percent in 2008. Daily use has also increased; 6.5 percent of 12th graders now use marijuana every day, compared to 5 percent in the mid-2000s.[4]

Prescription drugs and nonprescription drugs are other drugs of choice for many teens. In fact, 14.8 percent of high school seniors abuse prescribed pain relievers and over-the-counter medications like cough suppressants.[5]

Another drug many teens abuse is called "bath salts"—a drug that has nothing to do with the products used in the bathtub! Bath salts are synthetic drugs containing methylenedioxypyrovalerone (MDPV). They're usually inhaled or injected.

Shoplifting is another addiction. Shoplifters help themselves to about $13 billion worth of goods. Kids and teens make up 25 percent of today's 27 million shoplifters. Many adult shoplifters began stealing when they were teens. The "high" they get from taking something and not getting caught keeps them going back for more.[6]

God's cleaning power

God doesn't use soap to get someone clean. First, He offers us the possibility of a new life through the death and resurrection of Jesus. With the help of the Holy Spirit, we have the power to put off old attitudes and put on new, cleaner ones. Check out this passage from Ephesians 4, written by Paul the apostle:

> You took off your former way of life, the old self that is corrupted by deceitful desires; you are being renewed in the spirit of your minds; you put on the new self, the one created according to God's likeness in righteousness and purity of the truth.
>
> Since you put away lying, Speak the truth, each one to his neighbor, because we are members of one another. Be angry and do not sin. Don't let the sun go down on your anger, and don't give the Devil an opportunity. . . . All bitterness, anger and wrath, shouting and slander must be removed from you, along with all malice. And be kind and compassionate to one another, forgiving one another, just as God also forgave you in Christ.
>
> Ephesians 4:22–27, 31–32 HCSB

God makes us new inside by forgiving us of the wrongs we do. Confessing what we've done wrong is like taking a shower. We allow the forgiveness God offers to wash off the dirt in our lives.

If we confess our sins, He is faithful and just to forgive us our sins and to cleanse us from all unrighteousness.

1 John 1:9 NKJV

Don't just get cleaned up on the outside. Get clean inside!

WHAT'S *your* STORY?

Reread these verses below from Ephesians 4. After reading the passage, talk to God about it. What do you find most challenging about "putting on the new self" or taking "off your former way of life"? Write a note to your Secret Keeper.

> You took off your former way of life, the old self that is corrupted by deceitful desires; you are being renewed in the spirit of your minds; you put on the new self, the one created according to God's likeness in righteousness and purity of the truth.
>
> Ephesians 4:22–24 HCSB

The following passage is a psalm that David, the king of Israel and ancestor of Jesus, wrote. Is there anything you need to come clean to God about? You might make this psalm a prayer or write God a note.

> Have mercy on me, O God,
>   according to your unfailing love;
> according to your great compassion
>   blot out my transgressions.
> Wash away all my iniquity
>   and cleanse me from my sin.
>
> For I know my transgressions,
>   and my sin is always before me.
> Against you, you only, have I sinned
>   and done what is evil in your sight;

so you are right in your verdict
    and justified when you judge.
Surely I was sinful at birth,
    sinful from the time my mother conceived me.
Yet you desired faithfulness even in the womb;
    you taught me wisdom in that secret place.

Cleanse me with hyssop, and I will be clean;
    wash me, and I will be whiter than snow.
Let me hear joy and gladness;
    let the bones you have crushed rejoice.
Hide your face from my sins
    and blot out all my iniquity.

Create in me a pure heart, O God,
    and renew a steadfast spirit within me.
Do not cast me from your presence
    or take your Holy Spirit from me.
Restore to me the joy of your salvation
    and grant me a willing spirit, to sustain me.

                                  Psalm 51:1–12

CHAPTER 9

Dress the Part

Life is like a fairy tale. . . .

Ella clicked on the Pinterest link her fairy godmother sent her. So many beautiful dresses! *Choose whichever you like,* her fairy godmother had written in the email with the link. *I can get you that dress in an instant.* The choice was hard at first, but she finally settled on one that suited her best. Oh, it was so beautiful—the most beautiful dress she'd ever seen. And when she put it on, she felt like a princess.

PLAYLIST

"Video" performed by India.Arie (written by India.Arie, Carlos "6 July" Broady, Shannon Sanders)

"Be Grateful" written by Walter Hawkins

"He Will Supply" written and performed by Kirk Franklin

"Imagine Me" written and performed by Kirk Franklin

Clothes your way

If you saw Disney's *Cinderella* (either the animated movie or the live-action TV movie starring recording stars Brandy Norwood and Whitney Houston), you saw Cinderella's transformation from ragged servant to beautiful princess—all thanks to her fairy godmother, who whipped up a dress out of thin air. Don't you wish you had a fairy godmother who could do that? Imagine how cool your wardrobe would be.

How do you feel about clothes? Take this quiz. First, decide on your clothing style (circle one):

1. My clothing style is . . .
   a. Hip-hop.
   b. Average—what everyone else wears.
   c. Edgy and sexy.
   d. Conservative.
   e. Nerdy.
   f. Thrift-store trendy.

Second, circle True or False for each statement below.

1. Clothes tell everyone how I am inside.
   True   False

2. I would be too embarrassed to wear something outdated.
   True   False

3. I spend just about all of my money on clothes.
   True   False

4. I judge others by what they wear.
   True   False

5. I hardly ever notice what anyone wears.
   True   False

6. My day is made or ruined by the outfit I wear.
   True   False

7. If someone wore the same outfit as me, I would be totally shocked and angry. I want to be original!
   True   False

8. If I don't receive compliments about my clothes or at least envious glances, I get upset.
   True   False

9. I don't care what I wear, just as long as what I wear is clean.
   True   False

10. I dress to get noticed.
    True   False

11. I've never changed my clothing style.
    True   False

12. My wardrobe could use some updated pieces.
    True   False

How many times did you circle True?

Four or fewer: You see clothes as necessary, but aren't ruled by them.

Five to seven: You are average in your thoughts about clothes.

Eight to twelve: You are clothes-conscious to a fault.

The purpose of clothes

We all think about clothes to some degree. A new outfit, or at least a tried-and-true one in which we know we look good, can boost our confidence. Daytime talk shows draw large audiences with promises of makeovers that change average women into beautiful cover models. Just the right clothes and makeup expertly applied can be transformative. The ones who feel the makeover expresses who they really are inside smile radiantly as they come from behind the screens.

If you had to meet someone for the first time, which would you rather wear, a new outfit or an old one that still makes you look good? Many people will admit that when they meet someone for the first time, they want to wear something new—even though the person they meet wouldn't know if the outfit was new or old.

What purpose do clothes serve in your life? For some, clothes represent a life they think they want (for example, being seen as popular) or a stage they feel they've reached (for example, I'm no longer a kid so I shouldn't dress like one). For others clothes are a shield they hide behind. Things haven't changed much since Adam and Eve first tried to hide behind fig leaves

My Story

I was raised in a household where we were constantly encouraged to be different from our peers, so naturally I carried that over to my outlook on fashion and individual style. I was never one to focus on the name brands others wore, nor did I want to mimic the media's view of fashion, because I considered being a misfit a lot more ambitious.

I had the wonderful opportunity to attend a performing arts school, where I befriended peers from different cultural backgrounds—each of my friends being versatile in their own way. Over the years my personal style developed into a combination of timeless vintage and a quirky flair. I found a balance between edgy, feminine, and bohemian chic, all while maintaining comfort. I would like to think that my style challenges individuals to reevaluate the ordinary and search for something a little more unique.

Tiara

(see Genesis 3:7)! God made clothes for them (see Genesis 3:21) because the ones they made weren't very functional.

As wonderful as new clothes are, they do not make up for the grace of a humbled heart. First Peter 5:5–7 says,

> All of you, clothe yourselves with humility toward one another, because, "God opposes the proud but shows favor to the humble." Humble yourselves, therefore, under God's mighty hand, that he may lift you up in due time. Cast all your anxiety on him because he cares for you.

It's not easy to clothe yourself in humility, but I have learned that the more we understand how very much God loves us, and the more we comprehend the grace He has demonstrated toward us, the more humble we become.

There is a false humility that cripples us, telling us we are not worthy of any good thing. This is *humiliation,* and it is not from God. But godly humility affirms that all good things are ours because of God's goodness, not our own. When we understand that God's love is unconditional, when we become aware that we can neither earn His love nor lose it, we are filled with awe toward Him, and it humbles us in His presence.

Applying this difference between humiliation and humility to our lives will clothe us more beautifully than the world's most fashionable clothiers and designers. A humbled heart does not ask for attention from others; it gives attention to others. Even this gift of humility comes to us from the Lord.

Put on a new life?

A recent advertisement on the back of a magazine read "Good girls go to heaven, bad girls go everywhere." That's the promise if you wear the clothing in the ad. Ever believe that—that your life is dull compared with others' lives? Ever believe that "bad girls go everywhere"? How much of your soul are you willing to lose in order to find out?

Many teens believe that they can put on a new personality or a new life simply by putting on an outfit that's the opposite of their personality. After all, many movies and TV shows feature shy heroines transforming into super-vixens. Usually the transformation begins by the heroine throwing off her glasses and putting on a sexy outfit to get the hero's attention. Bye-bye, humdrum life!

Has anyone ever given you advice on changing your life, starting with the clothes you wear? Maybe you long to be on a show like *What Not to Wear*—a show with fashion tips to transform your life. Or perhaps to be popular, you were told to show more skin, like some singers in popular videos. But the clothes you buy can't really transform you if you're broken inside. For real transformation, you need the clothes only God can provide.

Put on Christ

There have been many books on the market to teach us how to dress for success. But God tells us to clothe ourselves with Jesus Christ. What would this "putting on Christ" look like?

The apostle Paul explains how to do this in Colossians 3:12–17:

> Therefore, as God's chosen people, holy and dearly loved, clothe yourselves with compassion, kindness, humility, gentleness and patience. Bear with each other and forgive one another if any of you has a grievance against someone. Forgive as the Lord forgave you. And over all these virtues put on love, which binds them all together in perfect unity.

My Story

It was Easter weekend during my senior year of high school. I had been overwhelmed with senior projects, term papers, and preparing for college. So when I finally had a free weekend, against my parents' advice to rest, I decided to hang out with my friends.

While driving home alone, however, I started nodding off behind the wheel, but I kept driving because I had only a few miles to go. Before I knew it, I had fallen asleep.

Still fast asleep, I heard someone firmly whisper my name: "Brittney!" Remarkably, I opened my eyes just in time to avoid hitting a massive tree and a light pole. Instead, I struck a brick mailbox and a stop sign. There was a strange feeling as though someone else was in the car with me. It startled me at first, but later became calming.

The impact deployed my airbags, and though my car was completely destroyed, I walked away unscathed. I will always remember the comments I overheard the police telling my parents: "We just knew we were dealing with a fatality tonight." It wasn't until days later that I was able to reflect on that miraculous night and reexamine what I had actually felt during the ordeal. I will never forget the feeling of God's presence as He wrapped His mercy and grace around me. I will also never forget, I am never alone.

Brittney

Let the peace of Christ rule in your hearts, since as members of one body you were called to peace. And be thankful. Let the message of Christ dwell among you richly as you teach and admonish one another with all wisdom through psalms, hymns, and songs from the Spirit, singing to God with gratitude in your hearts. And whatever you do, whether in word or deed, do it all in the name of the Lord Jesus, giving thanks to God the Father through him.

Jesus covers us with His goodness and purity so that others see that we belong to Him. He offers an exchange with us: our ashes for His beauty, our grief for His joy, our rags for His garment of praise. He eagerly extends this great exchange so that we will become like Him and show the world what a kind and awesome God we serve.

When we enter a room, others should notice our countenance of peace instead of our dress. Our faces should shine with the oil of joy that results from knowing how much God loves us. Our words throughout the day should demonstrate God's grace in our lives.

Put on forgiveness

Forgiveness is the key for locking the door to your past so that you never return to it. Unforgiveness reopens the door to yesterday's pain every time you entertain it. As long as there is unforgiveness in your heart, Satan, the enemy of God's people, doesn't even need to bring new accusations to God against you. Your unforgiveness accuses you.

Think about coming home, hot and sweaty, and taking a nice long shower. Would you put the same sweaty clothes back on after you've showered? No way, right? Unforgiveness is like putting sweaty clothes back on after God made you nice and clean with His forgiveness.

I know. It's easier to say *forgive* than to do it. Here's more good news: You can always ask God to help you forgive. Through Jesus, you're now made new. He provides the forgiveness you need to offer to others. But He doesn't want you to put the same old unforgiveness back on, though you'll be tempted to do so.

At first, forgiveness is difficult, but it is absolutely essential for a princess to learn how to maintain this virtue in her life. I took my weakness and laid it once again before my Secret Keeper, admitting to Him that I needed His deliverance and protection from the painful addiction of unforgiveness.

Dear Secret Keeper,

I know that I should have gotten over these feelings by now. How could everyone be going on with their lives when I feel like a car stalled on a six-lane highway during rush hour? It's hard to believe that anyone could wrestle with unforgiveness and still be Spirit-filled. But it does happen to the best of us. Harboring unforgiveness is far more damaging than what the perpetrator ever did to me.

It seems as though I am the only one left rehashing the past. It is not that you wish anyone ill will; it is just a gut-wrenching feeling that you get when someone who caused you to question your self-worth never acknowledges the injustice they have done to you. They could walk in and a sunny day would instantly disappear, as if a storm would erupt any moment.

Sometimes, I just wanted to walk up to them and ask out of curiosity, "Why did you make me the brunt of your heartless babble?" And right before I'd open my mouth and insert my foot, You'd tap me lovingly on the shoulder and remind me that I was looking back at days too distant to retrace.

Perhaps you can relate. Maybe you've already opened your mouth and inserted your foot, and are now dealing with the fallout of lashing out at those who hurt you. Well, there is good news. It's never too late to make forgiveness a part of your diet. It tastes better than shoe leather! Take the advice of Paul: "Bear with each other and forgive one another if any of you has a grievance against someone. Forgive as the Lord forgave you" (Colossians 3:13).

Put on godliness, knowledge, and other "accessories"

Now that you're clothed in forgiveness, no wardrobe is complete without the right accessories. Peter, one of Jesus' disciples, writes about characteristics no believer should be without. These are like the apostle Paul's list of the fruit of the Spirit (Galatians 5:22–23).

> But also for this very reason, giving all diligence, add to your faith virtue, to virtue knowledge, to knowledge self-control, to self-control perseverance, to perseverance godliness.
>
> 2 Peter 1:5–7 NKJV

Like the best accessories, these characteristics work together and never clash. As you add one, you add another and another. When you put on faith in Jesus, you put on His goodness (virtue). You also gain more and more knowledge of Him. With that knowledge come other characteristics that the Holy Spirit brings out in you, like self-control, perseverance, and godliness—the desire to live life God's way.

So, what not to wear? Unforgiveness and bitterness. Root those out of your wardrobe, little sister. Add the "accessories" of contentment and perseverance. No wardrobe is complete without them!

WHAT'S *your* STORY?

Check out the following verse from 1 Samuel. God sent His prophet Samuel to anoint the next king of Israel. Tall, handsome Saul hadn't worked out and needed to be replaced. Samuel viewed seven handsome sons of a man named Jesse, thinking that surely the next king had to be one of them. After all, a king should be tall and handsome, right? But God had this surprising message for him, which the verse below shows.

Write a note to your Secret Keeper, telling Him what's in your heart. You don't have to hide anything from Him. He already knows what's there. He just wants to hear from you. What does it mean to you that God "looks at the heart"?

> But the Lord said to Samuel, "Do not consider his appearance or his height, for I have rejected him. The Lord does not look at the things people look at. People look at the outward appearance, but the Lord looks at the heart."
>
> 1 Samuel 16:7

What, if anything, scares you about God knowing what's in your heart? Journal about that.

CHAPTER 10

Face Those Fears

Life is like a fairy tale. . . .

Ella had to leave the ball by midnight. That's what her fairy godmother said. But she had to *get* to the ball first. But no one would take her—certainly not her relatives. And what would she look like rolling up to the ball on the city bus? She'd look ridiculous. But if she didn't go, she would regret it for the rest of her life.

But what if she arrived and the prince laughed at her? What if everyone laughed at her—like they laughed when they found out how Josh had humiliated her?

PLAYLIST

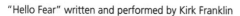

"Hello Fear" written and performed by Kirk Franklin

"One Thing Remains" performed by Kristian Stanfill (written by Christa Black, Brian Johnson, Jeremy Riddle)

"I Will Rise" performed by Chris Tomlin (written by Chris Tomlin, Jesse Reeves, Louie Giglio, Matt Maher)

"The Battle Is the Lord's" performed by Yolanda Adams (written by Varn Michael McKay)

"Breathe" performed by Michael W. Smith (written by Mark Barnett)

What do you fear?

Everyone has fears. According to the National Alliance on Mental Illness, 12.5 million people have a specific phobia of some kind.[1] The most common fear? Fear of public speaking—glossophobia.

Some reality television shows discuss other common fears like arachnophobia (fear of spiders) or acrophobia (fear of heights) while forcing those who suffer from them to face their fears in controversial ways.

Many teens admit to various fears. How about you?

Let's take a look at some common fears among teens. One researcher came up with the following top-ten list:

10. No happy marriage and family in the future
9. AIDS
8. Premarital sex being a requirement for acceptance by the opposite sex
7. Lack of time during the day
6. Not knowing right from wrong
5. Peer pressure
4. Violent crime
3. Financial issues (joblessness)
2. Inability to get a good education (won't get into college)
1. Something bad might happen to a family member[2]

Other surveys of teens mention the same fears. Some cite joblessness and violence as the top fears of teens. Another study found that 46 percent of teens fear risk taking—a necessary component in problem solving. Why? They fear failure, due to high expectations of family members.[3] Can you relate? Are any of these fears yours? We live in an age where school shootings and other acts of violence are a sad reality—a consequence of a broken world. Another consequence is the economic recession. The divide between the haves and the have-nots grows wider. With many teens competing for college scholarships, some teens fear that they won't have the opportunity to go to college. Consequently, they fear the future.

Shaped by the past

Sometimes life brands you in such a way that you remain in a state of fear. Crimes like physical abuse, sexual assault, stalking, bullying, and cyberbullying rob their victims in many ways. One of them is an erosion of trust and safety.

The U.S. Department of Justice lists these statistics on sexual assault for the years 2005–2010:

- Some of the highest rates of sexual violence were against women and girls under the age of thirty-five who lived in lower-income households and who lived in rural areas.
- In 11 percent of rape or sexual assault victimizations, the offender was armed with a gun, knife, or other weapon.
- In 78 percent of sexual violence cases, the offender was a family member, intimate partner, friend, or acquaintance.[4]

Many victims of rape also find their reputations damaged. "She must have asked for it somehow," callous individuals claim. Such a lie adds further emotional damage and further erosion of trust. The path to healing requires support from others. But because of the shame and condemnation, many victims of rape are tempted to hide away.

As for bullying, 28 percent of students aged twelve to eighteen admitted to being bullied at school.[5] With many students carrying guns and other weapons, school is sometimes a very dangerous place.

But cyberbullying can happen within your own home as you check your email or social media, thanks to hateful messages sent by cyberstalkers. Approximately 9 percent of tweens and teens have been bullied online.[6] Has this happened to you? Although many states have banned cyberbullying, cyberbullies or parents of cyberbullies so far cannot be prosecuted directly for it. But laws are slowly changing. I'll talk more about one of the sad consequences of bullying and cyberbullying in the next chapter.

Chances are, you might know someone who has been victimized in one of the above ways. Perhaps you are that someone. And perhaps you wonder where God was when the incident occurred.

Oh, daughter, God can rebuild your life from the inside out. He can replace your fear, shame, and loss with His security and clothe you with His love. Will you let Him?

My Story

I can relate to fears about failure, violence, the future. . . . I guess something to add (for me personally) is a fear of wasting my life, looking back and seeing that I really didn't do anything that mattered. That my life meant nothing. Violent crime is also a big fear among me and my friends, especially now with all the shootings and the publicized kidnappings and gruesome circumstances surrounding those. More so than being afraid that something like that will happen to me, I worry that something awful will happen to my younger brother or sister.

God has responded to that by calming my worries and revealing to me that things will be okay if I take it one day at a time.

Hannah

WHAT'S *your* STORY?

Read the following verse. How does it make you feel, knowing that God wants to help you? In what ways do you need His help?

So do not fear, for I am with you; do not be dismayed, for I am your God. I will strengthen you and help you; I will uphold you with my righteous right hand.

Isaiah 41:10

Is there a friend or family member who needs God's strength or comfort? Sometimes God uses people to make a difference in someone's life, especially people who have been through hard times. Journal about the ways you are willing to be used by God.

CHAPTER 11

You Fit Right In

Life is like a fairy tale. . . .

As Ella opened the doors of the ballroom, music and laughter filled the room. Everyone seemed to be having a wonderful time. But instead of striding down the stairs leading to the ballroom, Ella hovered anxiously by the doors. When she left home, she was sure she looked her best. But here, everyone seemed to be dressed finer than she. Yet no one was finer dressed than the prince.

There he was at the bottom of the stairs greeting people. She felt suddenly shy. How could she ever have thought that she could fit in here? Maybe it wasn't too late to go home. Perhaps she needed to check her makeup in the restroom mirror.

PLAYLIST

"Open My Heart" performed by Yolanda Adams (written by Yolanda Adams, James Harris, James "Big Jim" Wright, Terry Lewis)

"What Love Really Means" performed by J. J. Heller (written by J. J. Heller and Dave Heller)

Trying to fit

You've got a crew, right? Friends you hang out with? Places where you like to hang? Even if you don't have a posse, you've probably got a friend or two who remind you that you fit right in.

Yet many teens struggle to fit in. Some feel isolated due to shyness or fear of not measuring up. Still others struggle with issues beyond their control—like autism spectrum disorder, which includes Asperger's syndrome, or attention deficit hyperactivity disorder (ADHD). One in 88 kids has been diagnosed with autism spectrum disorder,[1] and 8.4 percent of kids ages three to

My Story

Many times in my life I felt as if I was not good enough to hang out with or be in a certain group with certain people—whether at school, at church, or anywhere, for that matter. Instead of just being myself, I would say, act, and do different things I thought would make me seem worthy or cool enough to "fit in." I was afraid that being myself was not good enough for who they were, or that I would get made fun of and not be accepted. So I just did what I thought would work. I hid the real me behind the me that I imagined was cool enough. But in reality, day by day, it made me feel more and more isolated because I knew I was being fake. All of my insecurities revealed more than what I was trying to show. And all along, all they wanted was the real me in the first place. So I realized that I would never fit in, no matter how hard I acted or tried, if I couldn't be myself.

Darnesha

seventeen have ADHD.[2] So more than likely you know someone who struggles with one of these challenges.

To some degree or other, all of us have the fear of fitting in. Sometimes we're afraid to let others see what we're like, fearing they'll reject us if they knew the "real" us. We put up a front, trying to fit in, trying to survive.

Depression: the great divider

When life doesn't seem to be going your way, do you ever feel down? Many people do, and are able to conquer these feelings fairly quickly. Yet many also have admitted to feelings of depression that don't seem to go away. Depression is a big ball of sadness, helplessness, and hopelessness. So how do you know if you're depressed? Here are some of the signs:

- The feeling doesn't go away.
- You lose interest in normal activities.
- You sleep too much or too little.
- You have difficulty concentrating.

And there are others listed at WebMD.[3] The thing of it is, you can't make the feelings go away at the snap of a finger, though well-meaning people might tell you to "snap out of it."

The Old Testament prophet Elijah was no stranger to depression. When Queen Jezebel threatened to kill him, Elijah ran for his life. All Elijah wanted to do was die. But God dealt with Elijah practically and patiently.

Elijah was afraid and ran for his life. When he came to Beersheba in Judah, he left his servant there, while he himself went a day's journey into the wilderness. He came to a broom bush, sat down under it and prayed that he might die. "I have had enough, Lord," he said. "Take my life; I am no better than my ancestors." Then he lay down under the bush and fell asleep.

All at once an angel touched him and said, "Get up and eat." He looked around, and there by his head was some bread baked over hot coals, and a jar of water. He ate and drank and then lay down again.

The angel of the Lord came back a second time and touched him and said, "Get up and eat, for the journey is too much for you." So he got up and ate and drank. Strengthened by that food, he traveled forty days and forty nights until he reached Horeb, the mountain of God. There he went into a cave and spent the night.

1 Kings 19:3–9

Later, God spoke with Elijah in a gentle manner, never once scolding Elijah.

The Lord said, "Go out and stand on the mountain in the presence of the Lord, for the Lord is about to pass by."

Then a great and powerful wind tore the mountains apart and shattered the rocks before the Lord, but the Lord was not in the wind. After the wind there was an earthquake, but the Lord was not in the earthquake. After the earthquake came a fire, but the Lord was not in the fire. And after the fire came a gentle whisper. When Elijah heard it, he pulled his cloak over his face and went out and stood at the mouth of the cave.

1 Kings 19:11–13

Has anyone ever treated you this way? Are you wishing someone would? If you're feeling depressed, don't hide it. Tell someone who cares. God is the one who cares more than anyone. Tell Him everything you're feeling. Don't hold back. He can handle it.

118

Sometimes rest is the best medicine to help you regain your strength. For severe depression, some doctors recommend antidepressants. But that's something to discuss with your family and your doctor. In the meantime, God invites you to lean heavily on Him.

> But those who trust in the Lord will renew their strength; they will soar on wings like eagles; they will run and not grow weary; they will walk and not faint.
>
> Isaiah 40:31 HCSB

The downward slide to suicide

When depression isn't treated, some have continued on the downward slide toward thoughts of suicide. The American Psychological Association lists suicide as the third leading cause of death for fifteen- to twenty-four-year-olds. One in 12 teens has attempted to commit suicide.[4] Sadly, the suicide rate has climbed. Females outnumber males in attempted suicide.

Many attempted suicide because they were bullied. Some succeed in their attempt. Some were egged on by callous individuals who sent damaging texts, daring them to do it. In 2013, you probably heard the sad story of a twelve-year-old girl in Florida who committed suicide as a result of being bullied online. Two young people were arrested for aggravated stalking in this case.[5]

People who are suicidal don't always talk about their feelings. Here are some of the warning signs of suicide:

- Talking of dying
- A recent loss
- Sadness or irritability—changes in personality
- Behavior change

- Sleep pattern change
- Appetite loss
- Erratic behavior
- Low self-esteem
- No hope for the future[6]

If you struggle with thoughts of suicide, believing no one cares and there's no way out, I urge you not to give up, beloved daughter. Seek help. Call one of the numbers on page 197. Someone is waiting to listen. If you're being bullied, tell someone. Don't keep it a secret.

That awful anxiety

Another way people feel left out is through anxiety. Millions of people in this country have anxiety to some extent.

There are different types and levels of anxiety: phobias, obsessive compulsive disorder (OCD), panic attacks, post-traumatic stress, and others. Some are more severe than others.

About 8 percent of teens (ages thirteen through eighteen) have an anxiety disorder.[7] To get the help they need, many turn to therapy or medication. But for others, such treatment is totally out of reach financially. So they go untreated.

In one of His most well-known sermons—the Sermon on the Mount—Jesus addressed anxiety:

> Therefore I tell you, do not worry about your life, what you will eat or drink; or about your body, what you will wear. Is not life more than food, and the body more than clothes? Look at the birds of the air; they do not sow or reap or store away in barns, and yet your heavenly Father feeds them. Are you not much more valuable than they? Can any one of you by worrying add a single hour to your life?

And why do you worry about clothes? See how the flowers of the field grow. They do not labor or spin. Yet I tell you that not even Solomon in all his splendor was dressed like one of these. If that is how God clothes the grass of the field, which is here today and tomorrow is thrown into the fire, will he not much more clothe you—you of little faith? So do not worry, saying, "What shall we eat?" or "What shall we drink?" or "What shall we wear?" For the pagans run after all these things, and your heavenly Father knows that you need them. But seek first his kingdom and his righteousness, and all these things will be given to you as well. Therefore do not worry about tomorrow, for tomorrow will worry about itself. Each day has enough trouble of its own.

Matthew 6:25–34

Paul the apostle also provides good advice:

Don't worry about anything, but in everything, through prayer and petition with thanksgiving, let your requests be made known to God. And the peace of God, which surpasses every thought, will guard your hearts and minds in Christ Jesus.

Philippians 4:6–7 HCSB

Pretty words, huh? But perhaps you just aren't feeling them. You don't have to pretend. God can help you. Prayer plus the power of God's Word provides the one-two punch you need to combat anxious thoughts.

I won't pretend that getting through anxiety is easy. It isn't. But with God, you can get through it.

The seeker

Jesus knew all about people on the fringe. He deliberately searched for those who were left out. We see Him searching for someone who was hiding when He went through Samaria on His way to Galilee. John, one of His disciples, recorded the story (John 4).

Going through Samaria was the shortest way. But Samaria was normally avoided by Jews. You see, the Jews and the Samaritans didn't get along. The Samaritans were descendants of Israelites in the northern kingdom of Israel. But they had intermarried with Gentiles (non-Jews). Uncool, according to the Jews.

However, Jesus was not like the other Jews. He decided that He must go through Samaria on this particular day. I like the way the King James Version states it: "And he must needs go through Samaria." Another translation says, "It was necessary for Him to go through Samaria" (AMP).

I believe it was *necessary* so Jesus could invite a certain woman at Jacob's well to be part of His family, which also illustrates His love for you and me. It was necessary for Jesus to meet this particular woman so that we could understand that His offer of salvation and hope is open to people on the fringe—people others overlook. Jesus wanted this Samaritan woman to know that she was included on His guest list. She was invited to drink from the rivers of living water He offers to everyone.

Jesus was tired from His journey, so He went to the well where this woman came for water. He knew she would come to the well at a time when the other women from the city would not be there. This woman didn't have a lot of money, or she would have sent someone else to draw the water for her. She was "nameless" as far as the story goes, but she was most definitely a memorable woman. She didn't have a lot left to offer anyone—after all, she had already been used by several of the men in town.

Almost everyone in Samaria knew her, but they usually referred to her as "that woman." The tone in their voice and the sideways glance of their eyes clearly revealed that this woman was not mentioned in nice family homes. No one ever walked up to her to say hello. Instead, they would murmur under their breath when she passed them, "Hmmm, who is it *this* month? Who is it this *year*? What are you into now?"

Maybe you know someone who has a reputation at school. You've heard the names she is called and seen the glances she receives. Maybe you're that person who is talked about.

This woman's secrets alienated her from the women who came to the well together. She came to the well that eventful day and walked right into the very thing she had been running from: She walked head-on into Truth.

A man was sitting at the well, and she had learned to be cautious of men who sat beside wells and found her alone. Such a scene reminded her of all of her past mistakes. Mistakes could have led to babies out of wedlock; mistakes could have led to rape; mistakes today could lead to new mistakes.

But on this day the man sitting at the well was waiting to let her know that she was not forgotten, and that God had a new image for her to wear. Jesus let her know that He knew everything about her. He knew about the man she was living with who wasn't her husband. He knew about the husband she had had before him, and before him, and before him, and before him. He knew the emptiness that these relationships had left. He knew she was the one who thirsted for something to quench the dryness in her spirit. He knew He was the only one who could quench her thirst. He waited by the well for her.

When she came, He asked *her* for water. Surprised that a Jew would talk to a Samaritan, she asked Him how it was that He would ask her for water. Check out Jesus' reply:

> Jesus answered her, "If you knew the gift of God and who it is that asks you for a drink, you would have asked him and he would have given you living water."

"Sir," the woman said, "you have nothing to draw with and the well is deep. Where can you get this living water?" . . .

Jesus answered, "Everyone who drinks this water will be thirsty again, but whoever drinks the water I give them will never thirst. Indeed, the water I give them will become in them a spring of water welling up to eternal life."

John 4:10–11, 13–14

Jesus knew what she needed: compassion instead of condemnation. She needed to be seen, not for her looks or what she could do sexually, but for who she was inside.

The God who sees

Another person on the fringe was Hagar, a slave belonging to Sarai, the wife of Abram. You can find her story in Genesis 16 and 21. God promised Abram (later Abraham) a son. When Abram didn't get the son as quickly as he wanted, he had a child by Hagar at his wife's suggestion! But later, Hagar began to annoy Sarai. Sarai felt threatened by Hagar and was cruel to her. So Hagar ran away into the desert.

But God didn't let her wander alone. He found her there and urged her to return. Because He spoke to her, Hagar was overjoyed.

She gave this name to the Lord who spoke to her: "You are the God who sees me," for she said, "I have now seen the One who sees me."

Genesis 16:13

Hagar had her baby—Ishmael. But later Sarai, who was now called Sarah, finally had a baby of her own—Isaac. Sarah convinced Abram—now Abraham—to send Hagar and Ishmael away. But in the desert, they ran out of water. Hagar was convinced that she would die along with her son. Imagine how depressed Hagar must have felt. But once again, God made himself known to her. He pointed the way to a well of water, reminding her that He still cared about her.

The God who sees through your eyes

The stories of the woman at the well and Hagar show us that people on the fringe need to be loved. That kid who only comes to youth group every once in a while; that girl in your government class who never talks to anyone and looks down when she walks down the hall; the neighbor who goes to your school but only seems to have a few friends.

God uses people to show His love. Are you willing to be someone God uses to show His compassion? He comforts you so that you can pass that comfort along to others.

> It is because of the Lord's mercy and loving-kindness that we are not consumed, because His [tender] compassions fail not. They are new every morning; great and abundant is Your stability and faithfulness.
>
> Lamentations 3:22–23 AMP

> Blessed be the God and Father of our Lord Jesus Christ, the Father of mercies and God of all comfort, who comforts us in all our tribulation, that we may be able to comfort those who are in any trouble, with the comfort with which we ourselves are comforted by God.
>
> 2 Corinthians 1:3–4 NKJV

Feeling on the fringe? With God, you always fit right in.

WHAT'S *your* STORY?

Having trouble fitting in? Read the verse below and tell God how you feel.

> O Lord, you have searched me and known me! You know when I sit down and when I rise up; you discern my thoughts from afar.
>
> Psalm 139:1–2 ESV

Is there anyone who really knows you? Or are you afraid to let people get to know the real you? Journal about who you really are and why you have a hard time letting people get close to you.

CHAPTER 12

In the Powder Room

Life is like a fairy tale. . . .

Ella hurried into the women's restroom to check her makeup. Her heart thudded as she saw two girls already seated before the large mirror, combing their hair and adding lip liner. She recognized them from school. But their assessing looks told her they didn't recognize her. Perhaps they didn't. With her new hairstyle and killer dress, she didn't look like her usual self.

"Did you see that rag Iris is wearing?" one girl asked.

The other huffed a breath. "It was so ugly, I sneaked and took a picture of it. It's already posted to Facebook. I can't wait to read the comments."

While both laughed, Ella hastened out of the room. She didn't want to give them the opportunity to mock her too.

PLAYLIST

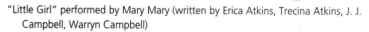

"Little Girl" performed by Mary Mary (written by Erica Atkins, Trecina Atkins, J. J. Campbell, Warryn Campbell)

"He's That Kind of Friend" performed by Tramaine Hawkins and Walter Hawkins and the Love Center Choir (written by Walter Hawkins)

Between us girls

How would you feel if you walked into the restroom and heard the conversation Ella heard? Have you participated in similar conversations? Maybe you know what it's like to walk in a room, see girls checking each other out, and hear them making catty remarks. Perhaps you've received catty remarks like that on your phone or Facebook page. Situations like this are the hard part of relating to others.

Still, relationships *are* an important part of life. God created Eve, declaring, "It is not good for the man to be alone" (Genesis 2:18). We were meant to have relationships with others. Friendship is one of the gifts God gave to us. A friendship is a relationship with lasting value. It's great being able to share your heart with someone who cares, someone who has your back.

Do you have a close friend or friends? Take this quiz to find out your friendship style.

1. If a friend needs you . . .
   a. You're available at any hour of the day or night.
   b. You try to be there, but only during school hours.
   c. You'll help even after school, but only when it's convenient.
   d. You'll help, but only if that friend has helped you in the past.

2. A friend swears you to secrecy about her eating disorder. But when her concerned mother asks you about your friend, what do you do?

a. Tell her mother what's going on. After all, you're concerned about her health too.

b. Tell her that she should talk to her daughter about the matter.

c. Lie and say, "She's fine."

d. Change the subject.

3. You have . . .

a. All best friends—you don't make a distinction between friends.

b. One best friend and a few close friends.

c. Several friends and acquaintances.

d. Few friends. You prefer to be alone.

4. When it comes to making friends, you . . .

a. Make friends easily.

b. Take a while to open yourself up to people.

c. Are friendly, but reserved.

d. Relate only to those who have the exact same interests. And that's very few people right now!

5. Your friends are . . .

a. Very diverse.

b. Only somewhat diverse.

c. Exactly like you (same race; same status).

d. Me, myself, and I.

6. Think about your closest friend. That friend can get you to . . .

a. Take a risk and see life in a different way.

b. Come out of your shell.

c. Do your best even when you don't feel like it.

d. Believe in the good of at least *one* person—that friend.

7. If your friend did something you believed was wrong, you would . . .

    a. Stick by her, but avoid tattling on her.

    b. Talk to her, telling her you'll have to turn her in.

    c. Think for yourself, refusing to be influenced by her.

    d. Avoid her from now on. Who needs that loser?

If you answered mostly As, you're Friendly Fawn. You're a friend almost to a fault.

If you answered mostly Bs, you're Careful Cara. You have friends, but they were hard to come by.

If you answered mostly Cs, you're Stick-to-Your-Guns Gwen. You know what you want, and you don't allow others to influence you—not even friends.

If you answered mostly Ds, you're Loner Lucy. You prefer being alone.

If your answers were a combination of As and Bs, you're Protective Pearl. You have friends, but you're also concerned about your boundaries.

For another challenge, ask a friend to answer the questions the way she thinks you would answer and vice versa. How close are your guesses for each other?

Friendship guarantee?

Quizzes like the above are often used as an ice-breaker activity. But the fact is, no quiz can accurately predict or guarantee friendship. Friendship is camaraderie you feel for another person. But every person you meet is not guaranteed to become a friend. Friendship is a mutual desire to work toward a relationship.

Ever have a one-sided relationship—where you or the other person does all the work? A true friendship can't be one sided.

In the previous chapter, I talked about fitting in. This is very true of friendship. Half the time friendships end when friends go in different directions. One friend seeks to hang with a different crowd, hoping she'll get what she lacks (popularity, a sense of belonging, being thought of as cool, a boyfriend she thinks will cherish her); the other is left behind wondering what went wrong. Has this happened to you?

Some friendships stand the test of time, but others end either because someone comes between the friends or because they simply drifted apart. Sadly, because of the fall in Genesis, friendships can sometimes be rocky. But there are sure-fire friendship killers.

Problems in friendship

Ever been betrayed by a friend, perhaps a friend to whom you told a secret and that friend betrayed you by telling someone else? Or perhaps you told a friend you liked someone and that friend went out of her way to make that guy her boyfriend. Betrayal is an acid that eats away at the foundation of a friendship. Once trust is broken, regaining it is difficult. Hurt settles in for a long visit.

Another problem is the loyal-only-sometimes friend. Maybe she acts like she's cool with you until her boyfriend calls. Then she ditches plans you made together, and you're supposed to understand that her man comes first. When he dumps her, she's back to being your friend. Or there is the friend who is only your friend when you have something she wants: money to spend or popularity rays she can bask in. She's gone when you have nothing left that she wants.

Unresolved anger, bitterness, resentment, jealousy, and unforgiveness are other emotions and attitudes that erode friendship. Unresolved anger often simmers at the back burner when a person feels used and abused by so-called friends who drop her like yesterday's news. Jealousy happens when one friend feels she's losing the closeness she had with another a friend. Bitterness and resentment sometimes follow a painful betrayal. They're like canker sores on the soul—very irritating. When you focus on the feelings and allow them to simmer, the divide between you and your friend grows wider.

Some teens have lashed out at others in bitterness and anger. Several school shootings are the result of harassed teens who saw only one solution for their resentment and frustration: killing others.

While bitterness and resentment don't always end in that extreme way, they're harmful in another way: They separate that person from God. Often God is being blamed for allowing events to take place.

That's why the Bible provides this advice:

"In your anger do not sin": Do not let the sun go down while you are still angry, and do not give the devil a foothold. . . .

Get rid of all bitterness, rage and anger, brawling and slander, along with every form of malice. Be kind and compassionate to one another, forgiving each other, just as in Christ God forgave you.

Ephesians 4:26–27, 31–32

God wants nothing to stand between you and Him. Anything that threatens to come between God and you needs to be removed; for example, anger that boils down to rage. He wants you to think of it the way you would think of a container of moldy food you suddenly found in the refrigerator: time to take out the trash.

Traits of a friend

We can learn from others how to be a good friend. In the Bible there is the story of a woman named Ruth. She has an entire book named after her. Ruth wasn't just a daughter-in-law, she was also a friend. In fact, Ruth's name means "friendship." She proved her loyalty—one of the best characteristics of a friend. She refused to abandon Naomi when they were both broke and alone. Instead, like a true friend, she stuck by Naomi and decided to return with her to Bethlehem—the unknown country.

My Story

In my junior year, I discovered that a person I had called a friend had been lying to me about the majority of things that I "knew" about her—about family members, grades, relationships, and more. After four years of friendship, I didn't know what else to feel except anger.

These feelings translated into a lack of communication for a month—glares and (when I eventually spoke to her again) snide comments that I was surprised I could think of. As time went on, my anger began to include feelings of hurt. I started thinking back to what I might have done to make her feel she had to lie to me, and when I couldn't think of an answer, I just stopped trying to get our friendship back.

One day at church the message was about forgiveness, and I felt ashamed. I had done much worse, and God had forgiven me; yet here I was holding on to my anger. It took a lot of prayer, but I eventually got to the point where I could forgive her for all of the lies. That doesn't mean that I trust her today, but I've at least gotten to the point where I can talk to her without filling up with anger. Out of all of this, I learned that forgiveness isn't always for the benefit of the offender (she didn't seem to care either way). Instead, it allows you to come to terms with an offense and move on with your life.

Jasmine

Are you that kind of friend? Friendship isn't just about what you have in common with someone. A princess for God is dependable, open, and intentional about maintaining a friendship.

Two of the best friends the Bible mentions are David and Jonathan. They became friends after David defeated Goliath and began hanging around the court of King Saul, Jonathan's father (see 1 Samuel 17). What's amazing about their friendship is that Jonathan had everything to lose by it. After all, he was the crown prince—next in line for the throne. However, he knew that God had chosen his friend David to be the next king! If you were Jonathan, what would you have done? Would you have kicked your friend David to the curb?

Jonathan refused to say *adios* to David. He could have wallowed in bitterness and resentment. Instead, he refused to allow anything to stand between him and his friend. Even his own father's poisonous envy, which led him to seek to kill David, could not keep Jonathan from making a covenant of friendship with David. A covenant is a solemn promise—almost like a contract. Both agreed to be friends for life.

Jonathan also faced his father's anger in order to save his friend's life. Then Saul tried to kill his son for defending David! (See 1 Samuel 20:30–34.) Jonathan's willingness to sacrifice his own agenda made him an amazing friend, one David cherished. Long after Jonathan's death, David remembered their covenant and took care of Jonathan's son Mephibosheth in honor of his friend. You can read the story of their friendship in 1 Samuel chapters 18–20 and 31 and 2 Samuel chapters 1 and 9.

Are you the kind of friend who is willing to sacrifice for the good of a friend? A friend who sacrifices is a true friend indeed. Jesus is the kind of friend whose willingness to sacrifice goes way beyond anything Jonathan did. He willingly gave up His life to show His love for all.

No one has greater love [no one has shown stronger affection] than to lay down (give up) his own life for his friends.

John 15:13 AMP

A gay friend

With more and more teens coming out, more than likely you might have a friend who admits to being gay. Maybe a friend has recently admitted to the fact and you're not sure how to react. After all, you've heard some of the Scriptures related to homosexuality (for example, Romans 1:27: "In the same way the men also abandoned natural relations with women and were inflamed with lust for one another. Men committed shameful acts with other men, and received in themselves the due penalty for their error") and wonder if God still feels this way today. Does that mean you have to condemn your friend?

Chances are, your friend has already walked a tough road of condemnation anyway. Many homosexual teens are the targets of bullying at school. According to one survey, about 26 percent of homeless teens are gay, having been tossed out by disapproving parents.[1] Some have committed suicide as a result of being bullied.

What your friend does not need is *more* condemnation. Pray for wisdom to be a loving friend. This does not mean you compromise your beliefs, however. It just means you relate to your friend as he or she is.

Other friendship advice from the Word

Being a great friend takes work. But you don't have to go it alone. The Bible has lots of advice on friendship. Here are a few:

A friend loves at all times, and a brother is born for a difficult time.

Proverbs 17:17 HCSB

A man with many friends may be harmed, but there is a friend who stays closer than a brother.

Proverbs 18:24 HCSB

As iron sharpens iron, so one person sharpens another.

Proverbs 27:17

WHAT'S *your* STORY?

Read the verse below. God wants to be that friend who "stays closer than a brother." Like any relationship, however, He wants you to spend time with Him.

A man with many friends may be harmed, but there is a friend who stays closer than a brother.

Proverbs 18:24 HCSB

James 2:23 says, " 'Abraham believed God, and it was credited to him as righteousness,' and he was called God's friend." How would you like to be described as a friend to God? Write a note to your Secret Keeper telling Him what you cherish about your friendship with Him.

David and Jonathan had a covenant of friendship. That means they were committed to their friendship. Is there any friend who has earned this level of loyalty from you? In what ways does this person have your back and you have hers? Journal about it.

Jonathan made a covenant with David because he loved him as himself.

1 Samuel 18:3

CHAPTER 13

Where the Boys Are

Life is like a fairy tale. . . .

When her name was called to greet the prince, Ella managed a curtsey, wondering if it was the right thing to do, remembering to smile though her legs shook.

His gentle smile caught her off guard. It lit up his whole face. "I'm glad we have this time to talk," he said.

Talk? Suddenly all rational thought left her head. They were supposed to talk? What could she say that would interest a prince?

He was so different from Josh. All Josh had seemed to want was her body. He never talked much when they went out. But the prince looked at her as if he could see inside her heart.

PLAYLIST

"You Are" performed by Kierra "Kiki" Sheard and Karen Clark Sheard (written by Angel Chisholm, J. Drew Sheard II, Kierra "Kiki" Sheard)

"Indescribable" performed by Chris Tomlin (written by Jesse Reeves and Laura Story)

"To Me" written and performed by Matthew West

Dude, what's up?

Ever wonder how guys think? Maybe you noticed someone at school or on Facebook and wondered what he thought of you. Perhaps you met someone and seemed to click, yet he blew you off the next time you saw him. Or maybe you have a close guy friend whose mood shifts like the wind.

As females, we can't help wondering about the opposite sex, what makes them tick. I talked about Adam and Eve's perfect harmony in chapter 4. But after the first sin, males and females had a hard time understanding one another, which makes relationships challenging sometimes. Yet we want them, don't we?

An old song has lyrics that repeat the title: "What the world needs now is love, sweet love." Would you agree? Millions would. That's why there are so many love songs, so many romance novels sold.

What would you choose?

Many want that Happily Ever After that fairy tales promise. What do you look for in a relationship? Answer the following questions to decide. Circle all of the responses that best fit your thoughts.

1. You want a relationship because . . .
   a. You're lonely.
   b. Everyone else has one.
   c. Having one is a way for you to feel loved.

d. You want to prove you're mature.

e. Other: _____.

2. Your kind of guy is . . .

   a. Just like Dad.

   b. As opposite from Dad as north is from south.

   c. Geeky.

   d. Kind and loving.

   e. Gangsta (not a poseur).

   f. Someone who acts like he's not that into you. You like a challenge.

   g. Attentive, but not overly so. You like your space sometimes.

   h. Possessive. You like to be cherished.

   i. A jock—totally fit.

   j. Like you.

   k. Like Jesus.

   l. A combination of these responses from above:

     A and C   B and E   E and F   H and I   J and K

3. To find someone to date, you would . . .

   a. Use a dating app like Tinder or Blendr.

   b. Put the word out through your friends at school.

   c. Get to know someone at school, then wait to be asked out.

   d. Hang out at the basketball court or batting cage.

   e. Hang out on Facebook, Twitter, or Tumblr.

   f. Hang out at youth group.

   g. Hang out at some other public place like Starbucks, the mall, or the library.

   h. Do none of the above, and instead _____

4. Your last relationship lasted . . .

   a. A week or less.

   b. Two months or less (but over a week).

c. What relationship?

d. A year or more.

e. It's still going.

5. If you had to break up with someone, you would do it . . .

a. On Facebook or Twitter.

b. Through a text, then delete him from your phone.

c. Creatively—like a message in a photo on Instagram.

d. In person—a screaming match in the hallway at school or in front of his home.

e. Other: _____.

6. In a relationship, what's most important to you is . . .

a. Compatibility.

b. Some chemistry; at least some light physical contact (kissing).

c. Major chemistry; heavy on the physical (includes sex).

d. Looks.

e. How others react to your choice of a boyfriend.

f. Other: _____.

7. On a date, you like . . .

a. To be in charge—to initiate when and where you go.

b. For the guy to be in charge.

c. To keep things mutual. You pay for your stuff; he pays for his.

d. Other: _____.

8. When you're looking for someone to date, you're really looking for . . .

a. A soul mate.

b. Someone to have fun with.

c. Someone who makes you feel cherished.

d. Someone who helps you rebel against your parents.

e. Someone who gives in to your every whim.

f. Other: _____.

9. How often do you expect to hang out with your boyfriend (outside of school)?

a. Every day.

b. Two to three times a week.

c. Once a week.

d. Only on the weekends.

e. Once every two weeks (we really are *that* busy).

f. Once a semester (we go to different schools).

g. Other: _____.

10. As far as the way a boyfriend treats you, you expect . . .

a. Respect at all times.

b. Some abuse. After all, they all do it, right?

c. To talk things through if you're angry with each other.

d. Obedience.

e. A and C.

f. Other: _____

I'll talk more about this quiz later. But first, let's talk about the ways many teens go about gaining relationships.

Are you flirting or are you just friendly?

"She's just a flirt." Ever hear someone say that about someone? Maybe you *are* that person, but feel misjudged. After all, you think you're just being friendly. Author Kristen Armstrong says, "While some people flirt constantly, others reserve this affectionate type of interaction for expressing genuine feelings that extend beyond friendship."[1]

When attracted to someone, many test the relationship waters by flirting. Flirtatious gestures include body language, glances, and words. Many see flirting as essentially harmless. Others see it as the first step to a relationship. "How else can you know if someone's interested unless you flirt with him?" some might reason. Yet sometimes people can't tell the difference between flirting and friendliness.

Flirting becomes a problem if you pretend to show feelings you don't really have for someone or if you flirt with someone to hurt someone else—for example, to make an ex-boyfriend jealous or to get back at a friend. There's also a danger that someone might misread the signals you're putting out.

Because people did not date in Bible times, there are no specific Scriptures on flirting. But the Bible has a ton to say on wisdom and not deceiving others.

> I tell you that anyone who looks at a woman lustfully has already committed adultery with her in his heart.
>
> Matthew 5:28

> Do not be quick with your mouth, do not be hasty in your heart to utter anything before God. God is in heaven and you are on earth, so let your words be few.
>
> Ecclesiastes 5:2

Does this mean you can't smile at the cute guy in your government class or banter with a guy you meet at youth group? It means you should ask God for the wisdom to be who you are without resorting to deceiving others as to your intent. Consider the consequences of your actions. If flirting is your way of gaining self-worth, you might be setting yourself up for problems in the long run. Only God can fill the hole you have inside.

Check out the last section of this chapter, "What do you value?," for more Scriptures to help you make wise choices.

Today's way to date: the Internet

In chapter 1, I mentioned the article "Friends Without Benefits" by Nancy Jo Sales. According to Sales:

> If you're between 8 and 18, you spend more than 11 hours a day plugged into an electronic device. The average American teen now spends nearly every waking moment on a smart phone or computer or watching TV.[2]

Does that sound like your typical day? Instead of meeting people the old-fashioned way—in person—many teens use the Internet to search for dates and trade photos of themselves. Has that been your experience or that of someone you know? They arrange to meet these virtual strangers, but wind up getting more than they bargained for. See the section "Older guys" later on in this chapter.

Meanwhile, some teens bare more than their souls at these sites. They take what they think are "sexy" photos that haunt them for years. Some get passed around by alleged friends. You might know someone who suffered through this shame. Perhaps that someone is you.

Many teens have a hard time believing they're worthwhile. So they settle for what they think they can get—even boyfriends who humiliate them online. Does that describe you?

A dead end

Another way some teens explore relationships is through pornography. Porn is not limited to guys. Girls are looking too.

> Porn is more available now than at any time in history—especially to kids. Ninety-three percent of boys and 62 percent of girls have seen Internet porn before they turn 18, according to a 2008 study in *CyberPsychology & Behavior*.[3]

Or this confirming stat: "Porn is proliferating, and children under the age of 18 have become one of its biggest consumers. Most of them have viewed it by the age of 11."[4]

And the *Telegraph* in London reported, "Girls think they have to look and perform 'like porn stars' to be liked and valued by boys."[5] Think that's just a problem in the U.K.? Think again.

The 2012 documentary *Sexy Baby*[6] discussed the hypersexualized culture that affects American teens and women, thanks to the cyberage. Facebook and other online sites were mentioned as places where teens strive to be liked and will do anything they can to be liked—even bare all.

Sooner or later, if you're online long enough—whether to play a video game or watch a show or whatever—you'll run into links blatant or less obvious that are gateways to porn. People will tell you that you can handle it. It's just an experiment, right? But some experiments are dangerous. Like fire, they can get out of control.

Pornography is and always has been a dead-end street. You can't find true love there. You can only find bondage. Many teens have become addicted to the images they see and have a difficult time breaking free of it. The best way to beat addiction is to avoid starting down that road in the first place.

Pregnancy and STDs

Another way teens explore relationships is through protected or unprotected sex. You may be told that "everybody's doing it" or "you need to experiment in order to get it right." But these moments of intimacy can lead to consequences. One consequence is an unplanned pregnancy. More than 300,000 teens gave birth in 2011.[7] Although this number shows a decline in birth rates, they're still happening.

Some teens have the belief that a baby will provide someone for them to love. But for many, a baby is more than they can handle. So they turn to abortion or to foster care. About half never graduate from school.[8]

A byproduct of unprotected sex is a sexually transmitted disease (STD). STDs include herpes, HIV/AIDS, syphilis, gonorrhea, hepatitis B, and many others. Some STDs can be treated, but some remain in the body for life. For others, like AIDS, there is no cure.

The belief that one can avoid an STD or pregnancy by using a condom has led many teens into a situation they later regretted. Be smart. Be safe.

Older guys

You walk into your chemistry lab and find a substitute teacher. But he's so hot, he sets off a fire alarm in your heart. You hear giggling and sighs all around the room as other girls check out the teacher. Some are openly flirting with him. Later you discover he's only twenty-three—not much of an age difference if you're sixteen or seventeen. After all, if you were twenty-two, he'd be only twenty-nine. You would both be in your twenties. So maybe a relationship between the two of you could work.

Ever talk yourself into a relationship like this? Many teens justify the "rightness" of a relationship based on arguments that seem logical. But such arguments are still a case of denial. After all, a relationship between a teacher and a student under the age of eighteen is *always* wrong. A teacher would court a world of trouble to initiate a relationship. Being fired is only the beginning. With statutory rape laws in effect, some teachers have faced jail time.

Flirting with a teacher might seem like fun, but it's trouble. Do yourself and your teacher a favor: Avoid it at all costs.

If a teacher flirts with you or engages in inappropriate and offensive behavior—and make sure the intent is clear and you're not being presumptuous—don't keep it a secret. Clue in a parent or the principal.

Now let's talk about some other older guys. Many teens meet and flirt with guys online, little knowing how old they really are. Even when they figure out a guy is ten or even twenty years older, they don't mind. After all, it's great to meet someone mature who's willing to spend time with you, right?

Wrong. Some guys online are predators, looking for someone to use. They hang out on social media and in chat rooms geared toward teens.

According to one survey, 30 percent of the girls who participated admitted that they engaged in a face-to-face meeting with someone they met online.[9] These meetings were arranged *before* they were able to verify the facts about the person they were meeting.

Just because a person you meet online tells you something is true, that doesn't mean it is. One man in Texas posed as a fifteen-year-old girl on Facebook in order to lure a thirteen-year-old girl to a hotel room.[10] She barely escaped a rape or murder attempt.

Be wise about whom you befriend online. Don't assume you can handle a relationship because someone seems "into you." Check out the next section for some great Scriptures to help you be wise.

What do you value?

Let's return to the quiz on page 138. What you value is revealed through your answers. Value yourself? You'll look for someone who values you. Think everyone's better than you? You'll look for someone who treats you as if he believes that—that he's better than you. Value God? You'll look for someone who values Him. But with valuing God, you get the added bonus of realizing your great worth too.

Sadly, for many teens, realizing their great worth is easier said than done. How you've been treated in the past affects how you expect to be treated. Thankfully, we have a God who treats us better than we deserve. This is known as grace. He is willing to show the high value He has for His people.

Jesus came to give your life a richness it would never have outside of His involvement. He makes this promise: "The thief comes only to steal and kill and destroy; I have come that they may have life, and have it to the full" (John 10:10).

Not only that, He calls himself the Good Shepherd (see John 10:11). This description is like that of God in Psalm 23. A shepherd's job is to guard the sheep from predators, since sheep are helpless. God takes this job seriously. One of the ways He guards His sheep is by providing good advice. God gives us His Word for our protection. For example:

> If any of you lacks wisdom, you should ask God, who gives generously to all without finding fault, and it will be given to you.
>
> James 1:5

> Do not arouse or awaken love until it so desires.
>
> Song of Songs 3:5

The first piece of advice is all about asking for help to make good choices. The second involves making the choice to avoid a situation that's too hot for you to handle. Sex is one of those situations. You'll probably hear people talk about how "everyone's doing it" or how you need to dump your virginity in order to get someone to like you. After all, that's what guys expect, right?

Abstinence is power, not weakness. And virginity is something to be treasured—not something to be thrown away at the first available asker.

You're worth waiting for.

WHAT'S *your* STORY?

Take a second look at the verse from Song of Songs. Tell God what you think about waiting till you're married to have sex.

Do not arouse or awaken love until it so desires.

Song of Songs 3:5

If you've already had sex and fear talking to God because you think He's mad at you or will scold you, don't be afraid to be honest with Him. God sees you through eyes of love, not eyes of anger. Read the passage below more than once. This is how God sees you. Talk to Him.

In all these things we are more than conquerors through him who loved us. For I am convinced that neither death nor life, neither angels nor demons, neither the present nor the future, nor any powers, neither height nor depth, nor anything else in all creation, will be able to separate us from the love of God that is in Christ Jesus our Lord.

Romans 8:37–39

CHAPTER 14

Where Did the Time Go?

Life is like a fairy tale. . . .

He was kind. Ella hadn't expected the prince to be kind. So when he asked her to dance, Ella froze like a Popsicle. But when the prince smiled so sweetly and spoke such encouraging words, she forgot her shyness. He was easy to talk to, and laughed a lot.

Ella startled at the eleven loud chimes of the clock. Eleven o'clock already? She'd been talking to the prince for hours. There was so little time left to spend with him.

PLAYLIST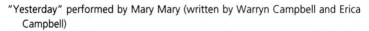

"Yesterday" performed by Mary Mary (written by Warryn Campbell and Erica Campbell)

"God of Wonders" written and performed by Chris Tomlin

It's about time

Time seemed to fly when Ella spent time with the prince. The joy the prince inspired within her almost made her forget that she needed to leave by midnight.

When was the last time you had such a great time? You never forget those times, do you? Maybe you wish time could stand still during those moments.

Some days, however, there don't seem to be enough hours in the day to get everything done. And some days, an hour can seem like twenty. Consider how long your last class of the day seems. Meanwhile, time spent with loved ones goes by at hurricane speed.

Scientists have determined that the part of the brain that measures the passing of time tends to compress the interval of time that has passed.[1] So events that seemed as if they happened only yesterday might have taken place three months ago. Amazing, huh?

In chapter 10, I mentioned that many teens worry about not having enough time to get things done. Ever feel like that? Many teens have packed schedules with school, sports, orchestra, clubs, volunteer work, and jobs. Not to mention homework, recitals, school plays, and other weekly commitments.

Is it any wonder some complain that they have no time to hang out with friends or just do nothing? Like them, have you ever wondered, *Where did the time go?*

Hurry, hurry, hate to wait

For some of us, we think our time is too precious to waste. We hate waiting—on files to download, on slowly buffering videos, on friends who are chronically late. We also want what we want when we want it—usually *right now!*

Another sign of our "hurry-itis" can be seen when we look to the future instead of the present. We think life will be better *if only*. Ever play that game? *If only I were older. If only he were my man. If only I had enough money to buy a car. If only . . . if only . . . if only.* The present becomes less enjoyable, because our heads are turned toward the future.

God wants you to enjoy the present—to keep your head in the game of *now*. But looking toward the future is especially tempting when the present seems miserable. *If only the bullying would stop. . . . If only my mom would stop hitting me. . . . If only I were old enough to be out of foster care and on my own. I hate the way my foster mom's boyfriend looks at me.*

At times like that, time seems an enemy, not a friend. Time weighs as heavy as a lead apron. When time is your enemy, you need a friend—God, the Prince of Peace. He's got your back, so that you can say like David, "But I trust in you, Lord; I say, 'You are my God.' My times are in your hands" (Psalm 31:14–15).

God is with you, no matter what. He also wants you to trust in His plans for your life. So when you're tempted to be angry and tell God to hurry up and answer your prayer, maybe you can ask Him to help you "slow your roll" and wait for His timing.

Time stealers

But sometimes, if we're honest, we admit that we waste time.

A habit can be formed when you do the same activity for twenty-one days. Procrastination is a habit that can be developed without much intentional thought. It is a huge time stealer. You put off writing that paper, thinking that you'll check your email, play a video game, or watch a TV show for fifteen minutes. Before you know it, you've spent two or three hours on the Internet or watching TV.

Okay. Honesty time. What are some ways you procrastinate?

1. Circle the ways you spend your time.
   a. Social media (Tumblr, Instagram, Facebook, Twitter, etc.).
   b. Video games.
   c. Texting friends.
   d. Hanging out at the mall.
   e. Watching TV.

2. How much time do you spend on the above each day? Come on, now, be honest!
   a. Less than an hour.
   b. 1–2 hours.
   c. 2–4 hours.
   d. 5–6 hours.
   e. Over 6 hours.

While procrastination can be overcome with effort, some activities, like getting drunk or high, require more than effort. They steal more than just time, they steal life. Those who indulge don't realize how much time has passed. But the minutes and hours start to add up. Time lost is impossible to regain. Not only lost time, but lost health, lost grades, lost opportunities.

Instead of letting time be stolen from you, why not guard it by setting priorities? You know what you need to do—what needs to be done each day. Speaking of priorities, here's a suggestion for your first priority: Spend time with God.

Lord of time

God is the ultimate Time Lord. (And you thought the Doctor on *Doctor Who* is.) Once, He made the sun stand still during a battle to allow the people of Israel to conquer their enemies (see Joshua 10).

God has a unique relationship to time. Peter, one of Jesus' disciples, wrote this in one of his letters:

> But do not forget this one thing, dear friends: With the Lord a day is like a thousand years, and a thousand years are like a day.
>
> 2 Peter 3:8

Though God invented time by setting the sun and moon in place, He is not ruled by time. In heaven, no one is bound by time. In heaven, eternity exists. That's forever time.

> For thus says the High and Lofty One Who inhabits eternity, whose name is Holy: "I dwell in the high and holy place, with him who has a contrite and humble spirit, to revive the spirit of the humble, and to revive the heart of the contrite ones."
>
> Isaiah 57:15 NKJV

But on earth, God works through time, because He knows we're limited by it. We have 24 hours a day, 7 days a week, 365 days a year like everyone else on earth.

Now's the time to set some goals. Maybe you'd like to manage your time better; for example, logging more studying time or volunteer time. If so, list your goals here or in a journal. Then as you fulfill each goal, list the result. Don't forget to include dates.

Goal:

Result:

Goal:

Result:

Goal:

Result:

Goal:

Result:

Here's a goal I have for you, if you haven't already achieved it: new life in Jesus. Daughter, I urge you not to take time for granted in regard to accepting God's love and sacrifice on your behalf. If you haven't yet acknowledged your need for Jesus, turn to page 189 and pray the prayer.

WHAT'S *your* STORY?

Read the verse below. What worries you most about time? Write a note to your Secret Keeper, talking over your day with Him.

Commit your way to the Lord; trust in him.

Psalm 37:5

What do you think it means to "commit your way" to God? How do you show that you trust Him?

How much of your day do you commit to God? Consider spending time with Him each day. You can do that through prayer and/or reading the Bible. Why not read through a book like the gospel of John or the Psalms. Make spending time with God a goal.

---- CHAPTER 15 ----

Kick Off Your Shoes

Life is like a fairy tale. . . .

The moment the clock began to strike the hour of twelve, Ella remembered what her fairy godmother had said. But she was having such a good time, she wanted to stay! After a slight hesitation, Ella ran for the door. She ran so fast, one of her shoes peeled off like a flip-flop and remained behind.

PLAYLIST

"Yes Lord" written by Armirris Palmore

"Kingdom Business" written and performed by Canton Jones

Your choice of shoe

Before we go further, it's question time!

1. What's your favorite type of footwear? Circle all that apply.
   a. Flip-flops.
   b. Doc Martens.
   c. UGG.
   d. TOMS.
   e. Converse.
   f. Vans.
   g. Jimmy Choo.
   h. Kate Spade.
   i. Hunter boots.
   j. Keen.
   k. Birkenstock.

2. What would you do if you lost one of your favorite shoes?
   a. Cry.
   b. Mope.
   c. Work an extra job to buy a new pair.
   d. Shrug. It happens to me a lot.
   e. Other: _____.

Rules, rules, rules

Everything Ella had ever hoped for was given to her, but on one condition: She needed to be home by midnight. Maybe that's a curfew you were given by a parent. Keeping that curfew might have meant you had to miss out on some of the fun those who could stay later seemed to have.

If you're a regular reader of fairy tales, you know that rules usually are given. Obedience to the rules is necessary for success or survival. For example, in *Snow White and the Seven Dwarves*, the dwarves told Snow White to never open the door to anyone. Well, she broke that rule, to her detriment. And in

My Story

The rules in my household with my mother are pretty typical for someone my age: Get good grades, clean my room, ask beforehand if I want to go anywhere, and make sure before I ask that I have good grades and a clean room.

The beginning of my junior year, I thought everything was going perfect. I had a new group of friends, and as a whole we were everything that any teenage girl would dream of being—pretty, smart, popular, fun, etc. But toward the end of the first semester, we started throwing parties. My grades started to slip because I was more focused on how popular we were than on adhering to the rules set forth by my mother. When you're the only one whose mother creates rules and actually expects those rules to be followed, it's hard to fight the flow.

I knew that I needed to be more focused on my work. But it honestly didn't matter to me. I didn't care. I slacked off the whole year—until I found out that the people I thought cared for me, didn't. Once I was in trouble, only a couple of those "friends" were still there for me. So I had to learn to get my priorities straight. I wish it hadn't taken me a whole school year to understand that. Now I know that the rules parents, teachers, and others set for you are for the benefit of you. The best bet is to follow them.

Khandice

the Grimm fairy tale *The Six Swans*, in order to break the evil enchantment that turned her brothers into swans, a princess was told that she could not speak a word for six whole years while she wove shirts for her brothers. How'd you like to have to obey *that* rule?

Each of us hears or sees at least a dozen rules or instructions every day. "Let's stand and sing hymn 212." "Turn to page 16." "Don't walk." "No talking." "Take out the garbage." "Soften the butter first before adding." Some rules are easy to obey. Some are harder. But you would obey any rule if it meant saving your life, wouldn't you?

God presented Moses and the people of Israel His instructions like the Ten Commandments (Exodus 20) and other commands. And in chapter 4, I discussed how Adam and Eve broke the one command God gave them. These rules were pretty serious, since disobedience meant death. But God wanted to shape a people for himself. Since He was holy, He wanted them to be holy—hence the giving of the law, and its rules for sacrifices and living a holy life.

These rules, like those in the book of Leviticus, helped stem the spread of diseases like leprosy (see Leviticus 13–14). After all, there were few doctors around. Disease could spread like wildfire. But God wanted to protect His people by reminding them to obey the rules of cleanliness.

Based on the rules given in the Bible, some believe that God just wants to limit the "fun" they think they can have. They call Him a "Cosmic Killjoy." Ever feel that way?

One of the rules people complain about most of the time is God's rule against sexual immorality (premarital sex, adultery).

> Flee from sexual immorality. All other sins a person commits are outside the body, but whoever sins sexually, sins against their own body. Do you not know that your bodies are temples of the Holy Spirit, who is in you, whom you have received from God? You are not your own; you were bought at a price. Therefore honor God with your bodies.
>
> 1 Corinthians 6:18–20

This is a hard rule to keep for those who don't like to wait. Perhaps you've heard someone say, "We're in love. Why should we wait? What if we died tomorrow? Am I expected to die without having had sex?" or "How do you know you're compatible unless you take a test drive?" Maybe you've said those words yourself. Others might ask you why God would "deprive" you of something wonderful like sex. After all, aren't we supposed to enjoy the things He created? Isn't sex one of them?

You might have heard others argue your freedom to do what you want to do. "You have the right to be sexually free." Movies, music videos, and TV shows bear witness to this "freedom." Celebrities are applauded for their forthright sexuality. Some are labeled as role models. But no one talks about the consequences of sexual "freedom," consequences like sexually transmitted diseases or fatal diseases like AIDS. I talked about those in chapter 13. No one talks about the guilt or the bondage to sex that some experience in the desire to be free from constraint.

At the beginning of this book, I mentioned that I wanted to prove that life is like a fairy tale when we put our trust in God. He guarantees that we will live happily ever after in heaven, and if we obey Him in this life, we can expect blessings today as well. Therefore, He sets before us the choice to love and obey Him. When we do, He promises to work all things together for our good (see Romans 8:28).

Don't get me wrong. Obedience isn't always easy. Others may mock you for your stand on abstinence and other aspects of living God's way. Also, times of testing come to those who follow God's way. The proof of this came when my husband and I suffered injuries from a deadly car accident. Here is the story of when I was a barefoot princess.

She wore one shoe

I can truly relate to Ella's leaving one shoe behind. I wrote a letter to my Secret Keeper about it.

Dear Secret Keeper,

It was as if I were watching a movie. Right before the impact, I saw the Jeep approach the intersection and prepare to make its turn. Surely they saw us. Certainly they wouldn't make that turn right in front of us.

But they did! My husband's cherished silver Anniversary Edition Trans Am plowed into the front of the Jeep. The battery from our car was projected like a bullet through the air. My husband's head cracked the windshield. My mother's shoe landed on the folded dashboard from the backseat of the car as she cradled my twin boys in her arms. The trim around the stereo knobs dangled like hoop earrings.

My husband beat against the door on the driver's side in an attempt to open it, disregarding the blood that trickled down his face. He kept urging me, "Get out of the car!"

I whispered to him that I couldn't. Before I knew it, he had climbed through the bucket seats into the backseat, forced the passenger door open, and stood by to assist us out. The boys were jumping up and down with the excitement only children can manifest. Mother, somewhat shaken, stood nearby while my husband stared with disbelief at my right foot. As he lifted me from the car, he saw the blood oozing from my ankle where the bone protruded.

Upon closer scrutiny, the ambulance attendant saw that my entire heel cap had been dislocated to the side of my foot. Without my saying a word, the nearly unbearable pain that I felt was evidenced by the tears that streamed down my face. They whisked me into the back of the ambulance with my husband up front peering at me through the window.

I felt the jolt of every pothole in the highway. They seemed to appear from nowhere to add more agony to my pain, as if it were possible. On the stretcher in the hall of the emergency room, I lay for what seemed like years. Nothing and no one could have ever prepared me for the words that the doctor on call spoke to my husband. He lifted the sheet, and with the compassion of an ice cube, informed us that I would never walk again!

Never is a long time when you're lying in bed month after month. But I thought about God's promises, like this one:

For the Lord is good and his love endures forever; his faithfulness continues through all generations.

Psalm 100:5

Months passed. I couldn't walk without crutches. I fell into a pity party. But my husband's love brought me out of it. It took hard work. Finally I could walk briefly from my wheelchair to the couch and from the couch to the table.

In a matter of time, love lifted me! My husband, my pastor, my friend taught me how to walk again! My confidence and my dignity were gradually restored. I returned to the tasks that I am so very fulfilled in doing: caring for my family. Every now and then, I have trouble with my ankle. But I am so thankful for the reminder of the Lord's miraculous healing power.

When I left my shoe, the Prince of Peace found it and placed it on my foot. Today I can wear beautiful shoes again. There were times during my recovery when other women we knew made cruel jokes about my crutches. I felt ashamed of my unattractive gait and single shoe, but I learned that I could walk barefoot in the presence of God.

But sometimes going barefoot is just the right thing.

Take off your shoes

When Moses stood in the presence of God on the mountain, God told him to take off his shoes because he was on holy ground (see Exodus 3:5). Perhaps God didn't want anything to separate Moses from His presence. Don't you think it's time to get rid of whatever keeps you from walking into the presence of God?

While you think about that, let's talk about the story of Ruth. Her story is almost like a fairy tale. Ruth began her life in hardship, like the princess in our fairy tale, but she inherited all the land upon which she once walked barefoot.

Look at her story in the book that bears her name. During a time of famine in Bethlehem, a man of Israel named Elimelech took his wife, Naomi, and his two sons to the country of Moab. His sons, Mahlon and Chilion, married two young women, Orpah and Ruth. But after a time, Elimelech and his sons died.

Broke and bitter, Naomi decided to return to her homeland and encouraged her daughters-in-law to go back to their homes to find husbands to care for them. But the young women didn't want to leave her. Eventually, Orpah heeded Naomi's advice and returned to her parents, but Ruth said this:

> Don't urge me to leave you or to turn back from you. Where you go I will go, and where you stay I will stay. Your people will be my people and your God my God. Where you die I will die, and there I will be buried. May the Lord deal with me, be it ever so severely, if even death separates you and me.
>
> Ruth 1:16–17

So one daughter went back to who she used to be, and the other one, even though it meant going to a strange land, decided to follow Naomi. Ruth loved Naomi and felt that this woman could teach her the ways of her God.

When Naomi and Ruth arrived in Bethlehem, they were still broke. Back then, there was no such thing as food assistance. If you had no money, you starved unless you could find food. Ruth showed her willingness to work hard when she said, "Let me go to the fields and pick up the leftover grain behind anyone in whose eyes I find favor" (see Ruth 2:2). Gleaning was a way to provide food for the poor. God included a rule about gleaning in the law:

> When you are harvesting in your field and you overlook a sheaf, do not go back to get it. Leave it for the foreigner, the fatherless and the widow, so that the Lord your God may bless you in all the work of your hands. When you beat the olives from your trees, do not go over the branches a second time. Leave·what remains for the foreigner, the fatherless and the widow. When you harvest the grapes in your vineyard, do not go over the vines again. Leave what remains for the foreigner, the fatherless and the widow.
>
> Deuteronomy 24:19–21

Ruth asked permission to glean in the fields after the reapers had passed through. She came early in the morning and worked with only a little rest. But her hard work didn't go unnoticed. Boaz, the owner of the field, checked her out. He'd already heard about how she left home to return with Naomi to Bethlehem. Ruth's respect and love for her mother-in-law made a deep impression on Boaz. In fact, he invited Ruth to eat with his reapers and made sure that she was allowed to glean where there was plenty of grain left. He also offered protection for her. After all, she was a lone woman. Anything could have happened to her out in the fields by herself. She continued to work in his fields until the end of the harvest.

Naomi, recognizing Boaz as next of kin, knew a good man when she saw one. Boaz was the best catch in town. She instructed

Ruth on how to approach Boaz with her request for their continued protection.

When Boaz became aware of Ruth's request, he blessed her for the loving-kindness she continued to show her mother-in-law. He pointed out that she could have become the wife of any man she sought, rich or poor, but she wanted someone who would also look after her mother-in-law. What Boaz said to Ruth is very important for all of us daughters of the King of Kings to understand. He said,

> Fear not. I will do for you all you require, for all my people in the city know that you are a woman of strength (worth, bravery, capability).

> Ruth 3:11 AMP

Ruth was a noble woman whose humility lifted her to great honor. She could have returned to her homeland and quickly married someone who would provide for her. She could have married a young man in Bethlehem and left Naomi to fend for herself. But Ruth served her mother-in-law and offered to serve Boaz as his maidservant in exchange for protecting and providing for Naomi.

Ruth's humility did not belittle her, but elevated her position to the highest level that a woman in Bethlehem could hold. She followed Naomi and the God of Israel. In so doing, she moved from being a poor widow to being the wife of the man who owned the fields she had walked upon. She was brave, capable, and highly valued, yet willing to serve her mother-in-law, her God, and her fellowman. She also was the great-grandmother to King David, ancestor of Jesus.

Submit to protection

Let's look again at ways we can learn from Ruth. When she approached Boaz, she asked him to spread the corner of his garment over her, because he was her nearest kinsman and her rightful redeemer. *The Amplified Bible* says that she asked for his wing of protection over her.

Today, independence is a goal you're taught to strive for. Some will tell you that you don't have to be "chained" to anyone, especially to a man who only wants to lord it over you. Instead, you can be the one in control. Consider some of the televisions shows offered during prime time. Wealthy, powerful teens and women have their pick of hot guys—"boy toys." Here today, gone tomorrow, relationships as disposable as a razor.

But God wants us to be totally dependent upon Him. Eve's attempt to find wisdom apart from His guidance was the reason she fell from His grace. God does not want us to prove *ourselves* but to prove *Him*. His ways confound the world because His Word demonstrates that truth is the opposite of what the world teaches.

In Ruth 4, Boaz carefully followed the law in order to legally take Ruth as his own. There was another kinsman who had more right to her than he did, so he presented himself to the other kinsman first. The first heir forfeited his right and confirmed the promise by giving Boaz his sandal. The covenant of passing the sandal to the other symbolized the promise, "I will not tread upon your territory."

Then Boaz went to the elders and told them of his intent. This is where Boaz received a blessing because of Ruth. They said to him,

> We are witnesses. May the Lord make the woman who is coming into your home like Rachel and Leah, who together built up the house of Israel. May you have standing in Ephrathah and be famous in Bethlehem. Through the offspring the Lord gives you by this young woman, may your family be like that of Perez, whom Tamar bore to Judah.
>
> Ruth 4:11–12

The elders saw that good things were in store for Boaz if he took Ruth as his wife. Through her willingness to submit to the counsel of Naomi, the protection of Boaz, and the plan of God, Ruth brought blessing even to you and me. After all, she's in Jesus' family line.

> This is the genealogy of Jesus the Messiah the son of David, the son of Abraham: . . . Salmon the father of Boaz, whose mother was Rahab.
>
> Matthew 1:1, 5

Rules that protect

Do you see the parallel of Boaz and Ruth to what Jesus has done for us? When we submit to God's protection, He will grant our request because Jesus followed the law to legally win the right to be our Redeemer. He confronted Satan, who had first right to us because of the fall, with the price He had paid for us, and Satan could not object. He looked at Jesus and said, "I cannot tread upon Your territory."

We are under the protection of our kinsman-redeemer, Jesus Christ. Why would we ever want to live our life apart from Him? Why would we ever want to prove our independence from the very One who loves us more than His own life?

This is why God wants us to obey His rules. He gave them not for our harm but for our protection. So kick off those painful shoes, princess, and enjoy the feeling of holy ground beneath your feet!

> Brothers and sisters, I do not consider myself yet to have taken hold of it. But one thing I do: Forgetting what is behind and straining toward what is ahead, I press on toward the goal to win the prize for which God has called me heavenward in Christ Jesus.
>
> Philippians 3:13–14

WHAT'S *your* STORY?

Hate to wait? Write a letter to your Secret Keeper, telling Him how you feel. Read the following verse. How does its message encourage you to wait?

> Since ancient times no one has heard, no ear has perceived, no eye has seen any God besides you, who acts on behalf of those who wait for him.
>
> Isaiah 64:4

Read the verse below. How does knowing God has good plans for you help you to wait for His timing?

> "For I know the plans I have for you," declares the Lord, "plans to prosper you and not to harm you, plans to give you hope and a future."
>
> Jeremiah 29:11

CHAPTER 16

Sweet Dreams
Really Do Come True

Life is like a fairy tale. . . .

Ella woke up the next morning, wondering if everything had been a dream. After all, the dress she'd worn was gone. And the shoes. Had she really talked to the prince? Danced with him? Would she ever see him again?

Suddenly, her phone chimed—she had a text. But when she glanced at the phone, she was amazed to see the prince's number! He sent her a text! The text read, *Found a lost shoe. Urs? Outside ur door. Will u let me in?*

PLAYLIST

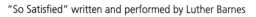

"So Satisfied" written and performed by Luther Barnes

"Never Give Up" performed by Yolanda Adams (written by Yolanda Adams, James Harris, Terry Lewis, James "Big Jim" Wright)

"Go Get It" performed by Mary Mary (written by Erica Campbell, Tina Campbell, Warryn Campbell)

"You Are" performed by Kierra "Kiki" Sheard and Karen Clark Sheard (written by Angel Chisholm, J. Drew Sheard II, Kierra "KiKi" Sheard)

Think about the future

The ball had been better than Ella could ever have dreamed. Her life would never be the same, for Ella had danced with the prince. Now she knew that no one else in all the kingdom could satisfy her longing heart. She regretted fleeing from him so quickly without telling him the truth about who she was. Never in her wildest dreams did she expect him to come looking for her.

When you think of the future, are you full of hopes and dreams or full of fear? Take this survey and see.

1. When you think about the future, what word comes closest to how you feel about it?
   a. Hopeful.
   b. Fearful.
   c. Indifferent.
   d. Joyful.
   e. Other: _____.

2. What are you most looking forward to in the next three to five years?
   a. College.
   b. Getting a decent job.
   c. Moving out.
   d. Traveling.
   e. Other: _____.

3. What scares you most about the future?
    a. Not getting into the college of your choice.
    b. No escape from your neighborhood.
    c. Still having the same old problems.
    d. Your parents splitting up.
    e. Other: _____.

4. The future will be awesome, if . . .
    a. You get everything you want.
    b. You have plenty of money.
    c. God helps you.
    d. You can beat this disease/addiction/grief.
    e. Other: _____.

5. What is your ultimate hope for the future?
    a. Getting married and raising a family.
    b. Living life your way.
    c. Being with Jesus forever.
    d. World peace.
    e. Other: _____.

Has anyone ever told you to dream big? Some people are afraid to dream at all, especially about the future, because they feel hopeless about the present. Some people hang out in the horoscope section of a magazine or see psychics hoping they can solve the mystery of the future. But only God knows the future. And He has a plan for you that starts right now.

Most people, if they would admit it, would say they long for love. They long to be "found" like Cinderella was found by the prince. Well, guess what. God came to earth looking for us to show us His love. He didn't sit on His throne and wait for us to find Him. He sent messengers ahead to let us know He searched for us. He sent prophets who wrote letters—books of the Bible—to describe His love for us.

He sent love letters to decree His intentions toward us. Finally, He came and knocked on our door in person. Jesus didn't care that we weren't dressed up that day. He didn't care that we were wearing our cinder-covered cloak of bitterness. He loved us anyway. As soon as He saw that we were happy to see Him, He swept us in His arms and promised to never leave us. What a love story!

And it is so very true! It's not a fairy tale at all! From the beginning of time, our Father has planned this story for you to understand that *you* are the princess whom He loves. He sent Jesus to find you, to take you as His very own bride, and to live and reign with Him in a kingdom where the ways of God's loving-kindness rule. He came to take you to a place where you will never cry again, or feel pain, or be hungry.

Is that hard for you to imagine? Can you remember a time in your life when you were happy? Can you remember a time when you weren't worried? Imagine feeling that way forever. The most wonderful part of this story is that it begins the day you say, "Yes, Lord, I will be Yours."

Jesus said, "The thief does not come except to steal, and to kill, and to destroy. I have come that they may have life, and that they may have it more abundantly" (John 10:10 NKJV).

Jesus is saying that He came to bring us the presence of God, and not just enough for us to get by, but more than enough, so the abundance of His blessings would overflow from our lives into the lives of others.

Let Him love you each day. When was the last time you let Him work out a problem for you? You can enjoy waking up to new mercies each morning. Jump out of bed to discover He has made your own dream for happiness come true.

My Story

Every day I think about the future. I wonder if it's really worth living for. I've planned it out and planned it out. I have sat and thought about all of the great things it holds, but at the same time, I question if I'll even get to see it. Each day it's different. Some days I'm confident in knowing that the future will be great. I know what God has planned for my life will fully go through as planned. Other days I just feel as if it really wouldn't matter if I got to see the future or not. One might think, *That's a sad and/or bad thing to say,* but it's the true feelings I have. You can feel a certain way one day and another the next day. Today I might feel as if the future is hopeful; tomorrow it probably won't faze me. Some might say the future is a privilege because we all know we aren't guaranteed the next day. To live a life and *hope* the outcome will be great, while fearing something will happen and you will fail, is the worst fear and feeling.

Shadai

Jesus can make you into a princess, and it doesn't take Him long. It may seem painful at first, because He will take things from you that you thought you had to have. But He *loves* you. He will only ask you to trade your rags for His riches. He will ask you to give Him your secrets, your filthy security blanket, and accept the radiant gown that He made just for you. What will you have to give to Him?

Ready to trade?

If someone tried to hand you something, and your hands were full, could you take what was given? You couldn't, could you? God has an inheritance with your name on it. If you are not presently enjoying it, there is something that you need to give up in order to receive God's best for you. Only you know what that is. If you have to think about it too long, you are probably missing the obvious answer. Nothing will stand out like this memory, this person, this habit that is keeping you from accepting your blessings from God. Maybe it's your dependence on a certain relationship, a certain addiction, or certain material things that preoccupy the goals of your heart.

What have you attached yourself to so tightly that tears well up in your eyes when you think about letting it go?

God won't share your heart with other idols. He will remove them from your list of "gotta-haves" and prove that you didn't have to have them after all. He will show you that you don't need it. You don't need that hot guy, that cool job, that popularity. You only need more of Him, and He will give you the desires of your heart (see Psalm 37:4). What an awesome trade!

Let's see. . . . I give Him my secret unforgiveness, lust, hatred, greed, and codependent tendencies, and He gives me forgiveness, love, provision, and transparency before all those who examine my life. What is this love that surpasses any fairy tale that we have ever read? Doesn't it sound worth trying?

He knows your needs

Don't turn back to your secret way of life before hearing how God can take drugs out of your system and alcohol off your breath. Yes, He will put you in beautiful gowns that won't come off for dudes who aren't worth your time. He will give you a new heart that will say, "I'm worth waiting for until the minister says 'I do' and a ring is on my finger." He will give you wisdom that tells you to get off the street at three o'clock in the morning. He will give you eyes to see that the person you are looking for will come to you like a prince, not as a thief.

The new heart He gives you will direct you to peace, not to poverty. God will teach you what is right and what is wrong. He will give you a way to escape from the evil that is plotted against you. He will give you the grace and power to do the right thing.

God confirms this promise in His Word:

> This is the covenant I will establish with the people of Israel after that time, declares the Lord. I will put my laws in their minds and write them on their hearts. I will be their God, and they will be my people.
>
> Hebrews 8:10

God knows your needs—not just your physical needs, but also your emotional and spiritual needs. He will complete the work He has begun in you. He will teach you to walk with dignity, as a princess. He will make you ready to marry a prince.

Trust me. I know. Check out the letter I wrote to the Lord:

Dear Secret Keeper,

Life, with all of its twists and turns, can be so unpredictable. I have always loved stories where ugly ducklings become beautiful swans. Little did I know that You were writing a similar story on the pages of my life.

I was born a coal miner's daughter. In my community, known as a coal camp, there were no big I's and little you's. Everybody was somebody because we all knew one another. Our fathers all worked in the same coal mine. When our daddies came out, all their faces were covered with coal dust. They all looked the same.

I graduated from our local high school with high honors. Off to college I went with no idea of what it was all about. I was so lonely during the early years that it is no wonder I ended up in the wrong company.

Soon the experiments began with cigarettes, alcohol, marijuana, and sex. Gee, how else could the coal miner's daughter fit in with these city slickers who I thought had it going on?

Through it all I knew that this was not Your will for my life, Secret Keeper. I could not get high enough to avoid Your voice, Your warnings. I would go to church occasionally and feel so repentant for my wrongdoings. I would have visions of walking past Mother's door and seeing her kneeling beside her bed. I knew that sometimes she was praying for me. Her prayers prevailed through many mishaps and calamities.

When He comes, your prayer may be full of unbelief, like mine:

Me, Lord? When I look at the way I was before You came into my life, I wonder, are You talking to me, God? You're loving me, Lord? Your mind is full of me? God, as holy as You are, You're talking to me! Not just every now and then, but on a daily basis. You've taken it upon yourself to speak personally and distinctly and call me by my name. There was no doubt in my mind: You were not talking to somebody across the room, but You were talking to me, God!

I was not looking for the Lord the night He rescued me from my cinder-smudged face and my pitiful corner of self-pity. Everybody around me was looking at me with expressions of surprise, as if to say, "He couldn't be talking to Serita. I know God's not talking to *her*." But the Lord said to me, "Oh yes, I called you something nobody else had ever called you. I called you forgiven, washed, holy, and purposeful."

Aren't we grateful to be saved, forgiven, and not forgotten? Though He forgot what we couldn't forget, He didn't forget us. He's already forgotten what we still regret. So many things happen to us during our lives that we wish we could wipe off the slate. We want to start over with a clean board. But the slate has been forgiven and erased. God did that for you and me, and we're the only ones who keep bringing up the past. We keep remembering who we were and who we could have been if we hadn't made certain wrong turns with certain individuals, but God is not thinking about that old girl. In the sea of forgetfulness, He's drowned her.

As special as He made me feel, I am obligated and privileged to tell you that He has the same love letter for you. He's a mighty God. Appreciate Him. Thank Him. Enjoy His presence and His sweet Spirit as He fulfills His purpose in you. Pull down strongholds, cast down imaginations, and put the past under your feet.

> Yet the Lord longs to be gracious to you; therefore he will rise up to show you compassion. For the Lord is a God of justice. Blessed are all who wait for him!
>
> Isaiah 30:18

WHAT'S *your* STORY?

Check out this verse from Psalm 37. Write a letter to God about your hopes and dreams for the future. What's His place in your future plans? Journal about them.

> Take delight in the Lord, and He will give you your heart's desires.
>
> Psalm 37:4 HCSB

How can you take delight in God? Think of some ways you can involve Him more in your life. Make a list. Don't try to play with God, however. If you're not feeling Him or think you're not, be honest. (He knows what's in your heart, girl.)

CHAPTER 17

A Prince Is Waiting for You

Life is like a fairy tale. . . .

Ella had a moment of doubt as she put her hand on the doorknob to invite the prince into her home. Surely he could see at a glance that she wasn't a princess. She didn't exactly live in a mansion. She couldn't pretend she was anything but ordinary.

What if the prince eventually grew tired of "ordinary"? Could she really trust that she could be with him forever? Even if she couldn't be certain of the future, maybe she could just take the first step: she could open the door.

PLAYLIST

"Something Big" performed by Mary Mary (written by Erica Campbell, Tina Campbell, Berry Gordy Jr., Alphonzo Mizell, Danny Nixon, Freddie Perren, Deke Richards)

"10,000 Reasons" performed by Matt Redman (written by Matt Redman and Jonas Myrin)

"Beautiful" performed by MercyMe (written by MercyMe, Dan Muckala, Brown Bannister)

Ever try to impress someone by pretending to be different from who you really are? Maybe you're shy and hope to be seen as fly and fun, but are afraid someone will call you out as a poseur once "the real you" becomes known.

Have you ever known someone besides your family who accepted you, warts and all? That's how you know a friend is a true one. He or she accepts you as you are. You don't have to clean up or dress up. You can be who you are.

When the prince learned the truth—that Ella was poor and ordinary—he was able to prove his great love for her by saying, "It doesn't matter what you have or what you have done. I love who you are. All that I have is yours, if you will simply say yes." He valued her above his own life and wanted to be with her forever. Together they served the people in his kingdom happily ever after.

Let's stop a minute and talk about Happily Ever Afters. In light of the problems you're going through, can you imagine living happily ever after? What do you think a Happily Ever After would look like? Take a minute and dream.

Perhaps you doubt you could ever experience the kind of unconditional love Ella experienced—the kind of love with no strings attached or hidden agendas. Well, you can! God *always* loves you, not just when you do something right. No matter what you do, no matter who you do it with, God still loves you. Does that sound like a love that only happens in fairy tales? But it's real! Only your secrets keep you hiding when He comes looking for you. He knows what you have done. He knows all about your weaknesses, but He also knows what you do not understand. He knows what the Father has in store for you, and He sees who you will become through your relationship with Him.

My Story

Every day I was constantly reminded of my mistakes, so why should I go to church? I didn't need another group of people judging me. Especially if it's the "mighty Jesus Christ."

You sin, you go to hell. These words were constantly said at my house. I was the black sheep of the family. It was all pointless to me. We were all going to turn old and die. Simple as that.

Weed and painkillers were some of my sins. I had a problem. If I went to church I would be a hypocrite. I wasn't a good person. At least, I didn't feel like I was. One time, I even made my brother bleed because I let the anger take control of me. I couldn't go to church. I just couldn't. I just faced the fact that I was going to hell. Malicious thoughts took over my mind.

So why did I go to church? Maybe it was my only hope. I went inside and sat down. I saw something incredible. Felt something undeniable. I felt loved. I felt my heart open up. As if all my sins were washed away. I was reborn.

Alanis

Don't let your secrets create walls that separate you from God! Jesus gave His life so that you could be with God forever. Instead, do as Ella did: Take the first step and open the door.

Here I am! I stand at the door and knock. If anyone hears my voice and opens the door, I will come in and eat with that person, and they with me.

Revelation 3:20

He wants you near

Let me stop a minute here and ask you a quick question: What do you look for in a fairy-tale prince? Yes, you read that right. Feel free to think back over some fairy tales you've read or movies you've seen. Now circle the traits below that you would look for in the ideal fairy-tale prince:

a. Handsome
b. Loving
c. Brave
d. Wealthy
e. All of the above
f. None of the above. Instead: _____

The prince in the Cinderella story was the ultimate fairy-tale prince: handsome, loving, and persistent. If you've read the story or seen the Disney movie, you know that he left the comfort of his palace to search diligently for the one who fit the glass slipper. Cinderella couldn't approach him without him approaching her first.

That's just what Jesus did for you. He left the comfort of heaven to search diligently on earth for someone to love: you. He made it possible for you to draw near to God.

Back in Bible times, only the high priest could enter certain parts of the temple to meet with God. The priest had to wash himself with water to enter the room where God was. Anyone but the high priest who entered it would die. A curtain hung before that room. It showed the separation between God and people. But when Jesus died, that curtain tore in half (see Matthew 27:50–51). That means there is no separation between God and people. Jesus' death bridged the gap. He wants you to draw near to God.

We are to worship God in spirit and in truth (see John 4:24). This means we must take off our mask and stop pretending that we've got it going on. Not that we could ever fool God! Take off the mask, and you'll see that you are in great company, for we all have had secrets. Let Him see the real you. Let Him see your pain. Let Him see your concerns. Tell Him when you are worried, lonely, or hurting. Let Him heal you with His truth.

He would never refuse to help you or leave you longing for somebody else to help. He will give you all you need. He always keeps His promises. He won't give up on you. He is a friend who will always remain closer than a brother (see Proverbs 18:24).

Please RSVP!

God is planning the ultimate party to celebrate the union of His Son, Jesus, and His bride, the church. Everyone is invited, but an RSVP is necessary.

A general announcement has been made throughout the Scriptures, but many people still have not heard about the party He has planned. Many of those who have heard don't understand that this party is very real. In fact, that day of celebration is closer to us with each new day.

The apostle John, who was one of Jesus' disciples, had a special vision of heaven. In the book of Revelation, we find our invitation to God's end-times celebration:

> Then the angel said to me, "Write this: Blessed are those who are invited to the wedding supper of the Lamb!" And he added, "These are the true words of God."
>
> Revelation 19:9

Peter, another of Jesus' disciples, explains how the RSVP works. (For more on salvation, see page 185.)

> The Lord is not slow in keeping his promise, as some understand slowness. Instead he is patient with you, not wanting anyone to perish, but everyone to come to repentance.
>
> 2 Peter 3:9

God isn't exclusive. Everyone is invited. And in the book of Revelation, you can see how many people accepted God's invitation:

> Then I heard something like the voice of a vast multitude, like the sound of cascading waters, and like the rumbling of loud thunder, saying:
>
> Hallelujah, because our Lord God, the Almighty, has begun to reign! Let us be glad, rejoice, and give Him glory, because the marriage of the Lamb has come, and His wife has prepared herself. She was given fine linen to wear, bright and pure. For the fine linen represents the righteous acts of the saints.
>
> Then he said to me, "Write: Those invited to the marriage feast of the Lamb are fortunate!" He also said to me, "These words of God are true."
>
> Revelation 19:6–9 HCSB

By grace, God delays the beginning of the dance in order to give us all time to accept His invitation. Great sorrow and disappointment await those who turn down their invitation to the wedding supper of the Lord. Luke recorded the warning of Jesus in his gospel:

> For the Son of Man in his day will be like the lightning, which flashes and lights up the sky from one end to the other. . . .
>
> Whoever tries to keep their life will lose it, and whoever loses their life will preserve it. I tell you, on that night two people will be in one bed; one will be taken and the other left. Two women will be grinding grain together; one will be taken and the other left.
>
> Luke 17:24, 33–35

Don't be caught like these two women! Tell God yes, today. There is room at God's house for everyone willing to come. We only have to accept the invitation, and all that God has to offer becomes ours.

Many people look at the coming of Jesus Christ as something far in the future. Is that how you see it? But you don't have to wait to accept His invitation. You can do it today! Know that God will be with you today, tomorrow, and forever.

> He Himself has said, I will never leave you nor forsake you.
>
> Hebrews 13:5 NKJV

You can count on that promise forever, princess.

WHAT'S *your* STORY?

Check out the invitation in the passage below. How will you respond? Write a letter to God with your RSVP.

> If you declare with your mouth, "Jesus is Lord," and believe in your heart that God raised him from the dead, you will be saved. For it is with your heart that you believe and are justified, and it is with your mouth that you profess your faith and are saved.
>
> Romans 10:9–10

Think back to when you first opened this book. How has life changed for you since you started reading? Journal about it.

What You Need to Know About . . .

Salvation

The plan. You've probably heard the word *salvation* used. It means to save someone from sin. So what does that mean? Well, because of the first sin—the sin of Adam and Eve in the garden—all of us were born with a desire to sin. Sin separates us from God, who is perfect and without sin. No one with sin can stand in God's presence. Even breaking one rule is a crime punishable by death.

> For the wages of sin is death, but the gift of God is eternal life in Christ Jesus our Lord.
>
> Romans 6:23

When God gave laws to the people of Israel to follow, they had to sacrifice animals in payment for their wrongs. Imagine having to sacrifice an animal every time you told a lie or broke some other of God's rules. The law showed how much people needed a Savior.

God, who is loving, knew that only He could save people. When the serpent tricked Eve into breaking God's rule, God came up with a plan He only hinted at to Eve.

> I will put hatred between you and the woman. Your children and her children will be enemies. Her son will crush your head. And you will crush his heel.
>
> Genesis 3:15 NIRV

God's plan was to send His Son, Jesus, into the world to die for the sins of all.

> For God so loved the world, that He gave His only begotten Son, that whoever believes in Him shall not perish, but have eternal life.
>
> John 3:16 NASB

> But God demonstrates His own love toward us, in that while we were still sinners, Christ died for us.
>
> Romans 5:8 NKJV

Throughout the Old Testament, God dropped hints through spokesmen known as prophets that the Savior was coming. They predicted where Jesus would be born—the town of Bethlehem.

> But you, Bethlehem Ephrathah, though you are small among the clans of Judah, out of you will come for me one who will be ruler over Israel, whose origins are from of old, from ancient times.
>
> Micah 5:2

The God-Man. Jesus' coming is known as the Advent or the Christmas story because we celebrate His birth at Christmas.

Jesus came to earth as a tiny baby. Why? Because He had to be human in order to die for the sins of all humans. He grew up just like you. But Jesus also was God. He lived His entire life without doing one wrong thing! Think that was easy? Think again!

A perfect sacrifice was needed. Back in Old Testament times, the people of Israel offered animal sacrifices for their sins. But they kept having to offer animals. A perfect sinless person only had to die once to satisfy the price demanded for sin. That perfect person was Jesus.

> He isn't like the other high priests. They need to offer sacrifices day after day. First they bring offerings for their own sins. Then they do it for the sins of the people. But Jesus gave one sacrifice for the sins of the people. He gave it once and for all time. He did it by offering himself.
>
> Hebrews 7:27 NIRV

> He did not enter by spilling the blood of goats and calves. He entered the Most Holy Room by spilling his own blood. He did it once and for all time. He paid the price to set us free from sin forever.
>
> Hebrews 9:12 NIRV

God invites us to admit our wrong and our need for Him. We accept Jesus' sacrifice by faith. That means we believe that Jesus' death on the cross—one of the worst imaginable forms of execution—was because of our sins. It also means we believe that He is the only way to bridge the gap between God and us. No other religion that you've heard about can make this claim.

> But to all who did receive Him, He gave them the right to be children of God, to those who believe in His name.
>
> John 1:12 HCSB

His divine power has given us everything we need for a godly life through our knowledge of him who called us by his own glory and goodness.

2 Peter 1:3

Now faith is confidence in what we hope for and assurance about what we do not see.

Hebrews 11:1

God presented Christ as a sacrifice of atonement, through the shedding of his blood—to be received by faith.

Romans 3:25

Jesus told [Thomas], "I am the way, the truth, and the life. No one comes to the Father except through Me."

John 14:6 HCSB

Having faith in Jesus also means we believe that after He died on the cross He returned to life, then returned to heaven. There, He is preparing a place for us. Someday, He will return to earth.

Your heart must not be troubled. Believe in God; believe also in Me. In My Father's house are many dwelling places; if not, I would have told you. I am going away to prepare a place for you. If I go away and prepare a place for you, I will come back and receive you to Myself, so that where I am you may be also.

John 14:1–3 HCSB

They were looking intently up into the sky as he was going, when suddenly two men dressed in white stood beside them. "Men of Galilee," they said, "why do you stand here looking into the sky? This same Jesus, who has been taken from you into heaven, will come back in the same way you have seen him go into heaven."

Acts 1:10–11

The prayer. God loves you! If you've never told the Lord that you need Him, you can do that now. If you don't know how to talk to Jesus in your own words, you can pray this prayer with me.

Lord, I need You. I am not proud of my past, but I realize that I do not have the power to break away from it without Your grace to set me free.

I surrender my heart to You.

I surrender my past to You.

I thank You that my identity no longer is tied to who I have been but with who You are.

I give You my future and choose not to worry about it anymore, knowing that You will lead me to green pastures and still waters where I will be cared for like a lamb with a loving shepherd.

Thank You for filling me with living water that will keep me from thirsting again. Thank You for removing my filthy clothes and covering me in Your beautiful robe of humility and righteousness. Thank You for dressing me as a princess and revealing to others who I really am.

With Jesus Christ, we can be born again. God creates new life within us.

Jesus replied, "Very truly I tell you, no one can see the kingdom of God unless they are born again."

"How can someone be born when they are old?" Nicodemus asked. "Surely they cannot enter a second time into their mother's womb to be born!"

Jesus answered, "Very truly I tell you, no one can enter the kingdom of God unless they are born of water and the Spirit."

John 3:3–5

This means we are new inside. God slowly changes us from the inside out. Check out Paul's words in 2 Corinthians 5:17: "Therefore, if anyone is in Christ, the new creation has come: The old has gone, the new is here!"

The Holy Spirit, God himself, comes to live within us. He is the One who creates the new life.

> I will ask the Father, and he will give you another advocate to help you and be with you forever—the Spirit of truth. The world cannot accept him, because it neither sees him nor knows him. But you know him, for he lives with you and will be in you.
>
> John 14:16–17

This is why God can make good on His promise to never leave you (Hebrews 13:5). He goes with you everywhere you go. He'll be with you forever.

Baptism

What it means. Have you ever been to a baptism? Perhaps you've been baptized yourself or have seen someone be baptized. But if you have no idea what it means, you've come to the right place.

Baptism is a way of announcing to the world that you believe in Jesus as your Savior. Jesus' blood redeems us from the penalty of our sins. The water of baptism celebrates the washing away of our habit of sin. Although we are saved by Jesus' blood, and not by being baptized, we are commanded by the Lord to submit to the act of baptism in the name of the Lord Jesus Christ.

If you have not followed the Lord in this act of obedience, I implore you to submit yourself to this wonderful ceremony He has prepared for you. Peter taught in Acts 2:38 that we are to repent and be baptized in the name of Jesus Christ for the forgiveness of sins. He promised that we would receive the gift of the Holy Spirit. In Acts 10:46–48 we see that even those who had already received the Holy Spirit were commanded to be baptized in the name of the Lord.

> Peter said, "Surely no one can stand in the way of their being baptized with water. They have received the Holy Spirit just as we have." So he ordered that they be baptized in the name of Jesus Christ.
>
> Acts 10:46–48

The power of baptism. There is a power that comes upon those who submit themselves to this public testimony that they accept God's gift of salvation. Through baptism we identify our past with Jesus' death, proclaiming that we are released from the bondage of sin.

Romans 6:1–8 explains what happens to us through baptism.

> What shall we say, then? Shall we go on sinning so that grace may increase? By no means! We are those who have died to sin; how can we live in it any longer? Or don't you know that all of us who were baptized into Christ Jesus were baptized into his death? We were therefore buried with him through baptism into death in order that, just as Christ was raised from the dead through the glory of the Father, we too may live a new life.
>
> For if we have been united with him in a death like his, we will certainly also be united with him in a resurrection like his. For we know that our old self was crucified with him so that the body ruled by sin might be done away with, that we should no longer be slaves to sin—because anyone who has died has been set free from sin.
>
> Now if we died with Christ, we believe that we will also live with him.

Water baptism marks the fact that we are separated from our past sins. Clean! Free from our indebtedness to the memory of wrongdoing! Water baptism is not simply a ritual that God asks us to do as a test of obedience. There is an authority with baptism that declares our independence from the powers that held us in bondage to our old nature.

Jesus was baptized (Matthew 3:13–17). When Jesus agreed to be baptized, we know He did it to fulfill all of the rules in God's law. We also know that the Holy Spirit came upon Him in a visible way after He was baptized. His public ministry began after this testimony of His submission to God. During Jesus' baptism, God announced that Jesus was His Son before the crowd.

Jesus was baptized so that His followers would do as He did. Matthew records what Jesus said:

> Whoever confesses Me before men, him I will also confess before My Father who is in heaven.
>
> Matthew 10:32 NKJV

The apostle Paul wrote,

> The Spirit you received does not make you slaves, so that you live in fear again; rather, the Spirit you received brought about your adoption to sonship. And by him we cry, "Abba, Father."
>
> Romans 8:15

> Because you are his sons, God sent the Spirit of his Son into our hearts, the Spirit who calls out, "Abba, Father." So you are no longer a slave, but God's child; and since you are his child, God has made you also an heir.
>
> Formerly, when you did not know God, you were slaves to those who by nature are not gods. But now that you know God—or rather are known by God—how is it that you are turning back to those weak and miserable principles? Do you wish to be enslaved by them all over again?
>
> Galatians 4:6–9

No, God does not leave us to fend for ourselves against our old ways. He gives us the power to be His daughters. Acts 1:8 declares,

> But you will receive power when the Holy Spirit comes on you; and you will be my witnesses in Jerusalem, and in all Judea and Samaria, and to the ends of the earth.

What a wonderful God we serve! Not only does He do all the work to save us, He does all the work to cleanse us. All we need to do is walk into His water and let Him wash away the cinders of our past life. Our old nature remains buried as we rise up to walk in newness of life.

Let me tell you my story: I can remember when I was baptized. I went to church as a favor to my mother. I thought, *Okay, I will go down there with those "sanctified folks." I'll go because I will still have time to get out and do what I need to do.* And as I sat there beside my mother, God's anointing began to fall.

I wasn't accustomed to the spirit of prophecy, so when Pastor started prophesying, I was startled that he looked me right in the eye and said, "You dream a lot. You have visions of things that are going to happen before they happen. God has a call on your life."

I started trembling, because I had known there was something I was supposed to do in the kingdom. But for some reason, instead of going left, I went right. Instead of going up, I went down. And instead of listening to the voice of the Lord, I listened to the voices of my peers, those who didn't know or care what was best for me.

As I sat there listening to Pastor, I became uncomfortable. I knew this was my day for deliverance. When he said, "Who wants to get baptized in the name of the Lord Jesus?" my feet hit the floor, and before I knew it, I was up front, bent over, repenting and weeping before the Lord. Afterward, the deacon baptized me in Jesus' name.

He kept saying, "Serita, look in the water. All of your sins are in that water. Look in that water. *Whoever* you were when you came in here, she's in the water. *Whatever* you planned to do when you left this service, she's in the water. God has put a barrier between who you were and who He has called you to be."

I looked in the water and saw dope and sex and a mess. I thought, *God, You did that for me? In a matter of fifteen minutes, You gave me a new life? How could that be? I was sick of me and You set me free.* Nothing changed outwardly. I still had problems that needed to be faced and dealt with. But my mind had changed. I knew that I was brand new in Christ Jesus, because He had accepted me just by my saying, "Yes, Lord, I am Yours." I started leaping and rejoicing. You can too.

Resources

If you need further help, here is a list of websites, organizations, and phone numbers you can use.

The Potter's House

- General: www.thepottershouse.org; 1-800-BISHOP2
- Youth ministry: www.facebook.com/bricked
- Counseling Center—www.thepottershouse.org/Local/ Local-Ministries/Counseling-Center.aspx; 214-333-6483
- TPH Insider (text message updates): www.thepotters house.org/National/TPH-Insiders.aspx

Abuse and Self-Abuse

- National Domestic Violence Hotline: www.thehotline .org; 1-800-799-7233
- S.A.F.E. Alternatives (Self Abuse Finally Ends): www.self injury.com; 1-800-DONTCUT
- Tips to stop cutting: http://teenshealth.org/teen/your_ mind/problems/resisting_cutting.html

Anxiety

- American Academy of Child & Adolescent Psychiatry fact sheet: www.aacap.org/AACAP/Families_and_Youth/ Resource_Centers/Anxiety_Disorder_Resource_Center/ Your_Adolescent_Anxiety_and_Avoidant_Disorders.aspx
- National Institute of Mental Health (to download or order a free booklet on symptoms): www.nimh.nih.gov/health/ publications/anxiety-disorders/index.shtml

Cyberbullying

- Cyberbullying Research Center: www.cyberbullying.us
- *Growing Up Online*, free ebook offered by NBC News: www.themoreyouknow.com/eBooks/

Drug Addiction or Alcoholism

- National Institute on Drug Abuse, NIDA for Teens: http:// teens.drugabuse.gov; 1-800-662-HELP; NIDA Drug Publications: 1-877-643-2644
- Teen Challenge: www.teenchallengeusa.com
- Substance Abuse and Mental Health Services Administration (SAMHSA): http://findtreatment.samhsa.gov; treatment referral hotline: 1-800-662-HELP

Eating Disorders

- National Eating Disorders Association (NEDA): www .nationaleatingdisorders.org

Homelessness

- Homeless Hotline: www.homeless.us/Homeless-Hotline .html

Mental Health Issues

- National Institute of Mental Health: www.nimh.nih.gov/index.shtml

Suicide Prevention

- National Suicide Prevention Hotline: www.suicideprevention lifeline.org; 1-800-273-8255

Teen Pregnancy and Sexually Transmitted Diseases

- Care Net: www.care-net.org
- National STD Hotline: www.cdc.gov/std; 1-800-227-8922
- TeensHealth: www.kidshealth.org/teen/sexual_health/stds/std.html#

Other Resources

- Solid Rock Youth Ministries (Real Help for Teens): www.realhelpforteens.com; 1-877-332-7333

Videos

- *60 Minutes*, "Gospel for Teens, Part 1": www.cbsnews.com/video/watch/?id=7361574n
- *60 Minutes*, "Gospel for Teens, Part 2": www.cbsnews.com/video/watch/?id=7361570n
- Dove Real Beauty Sketches (commercial mentioned in chapter 5): http://realbeautysketches.dove.us
- National Drug Facts Week Chat Day Video: http://drugfactsweek.drugabuse.gov/chat/index.php
- Brandy Norwood and Whitney Houston behind the scenes of the live-action Disney TV movie *Cinderella*: www.youtube.com/watch?v=c90CWobR5Yw

Great Bible Passages

The following are Scriptures you can read when you feel powerless, sad, or alone.

When you feel alone

Be strong and courageous. Do not be afraid; do not be discouraged, for the Lord your God will be with you wherever you go.

Joshua 1:9

The Lord himself goes before you and will be with you; he will never leave you nor forsake you. Do not be afraid; do not be discouraged.

Deuteronomy 31:8

The Lord is my shepherd;
there is nothing I lack.
He lets me lie down in green pastures;
He leads me beside quiet waters.
He renews my life;

He leads me along the right paths
for His name's sake.
Even when I go through the darkest valley,
I fear no danger,
for You are with me;
Your rod and Your staff—they comfort me.

You prepare a table before me
in the presence of my enemies;
You anoint my head with oil;
my cup overflows.
Only goodness and faithful love will pursue me
all the days of my life,
and I will dwell in the house of the Lord
as long as I live.

Psalm 23 HCSB

When you feel powerless

Fear not, for I am with you;
Be not dismayed, for I am your God.
I will strengthen you,
Yes, I will help you,
I will uphold you with My righteous right hand.

Isaiah 41:10 NKJV

But those who wait on the Lord
Shall renew their strength;
They shall mount up with wings like eagles,
They shall run and not be weary,
They shall walk and not faint.

Isaiah 40:31 NKJV

Finally, be strong in the Lord and in his mighty power. Put on
the full armor of God, so that you can take your stand against

the devil's schemes. For our struggle is not against flesh and blood, but against the rulers, against the authorities, against the powers of this dark world and against the spiritual forces of evil in the heavenly realms. Therefore put on the full armor of God, so that when the day of evil comes, you may be able to stand your ground, and after you have done everything, to stand. Stand firm then, with the belt of truth buckled around your waist, with the breastplate of righteousness in place, and with your feet fitted with the readiness that comes from the gospel of peace. In addition to all this, take up the shield of faith, with which you can extinguish all the flaming arrows of the evil one. Take the helmet of salvation and the sword of the Spirit, which is the word of God.

And pray in the Spirit on all occasions with all kinds of prayers and requests. With this in mind, be alert and always keep on praying for all the Lord's people. Pray also for me, that whenever I speak, words may be given me so that I will fearlessly make known the mystery of the gospel, for which I am an ambassador in chains. Pray that I may declare it fearlessly, as I should.

Ephesians 6:10–20

When you feel sad or depressed

My bones suffer mortal agony
as my foes taunt me,
saying to me all day long,
"Where is your God?"

Why, my soul, are you downcast?
Why so disturbed within me?
Put your hope in God,
for I will yet praise him,
my Savior and my God.

Psalm 42:10–11

May the God of hope fill you with all joy and peace as you trust in him, so that you may overflow with hope by the power of the Holy Spirit.

Romans 15:13

What then shall we say to [all] this? If God is for us, who [can be] against us? [Who can be our foe, if God is on our side?] He who did not withhold or spare [even] His own Son but gave Him up for us all, will He not also with Him freely and graciously give us all [other] things? Who shall bring any charge against God's elect [when it is] God Who justifies [that is, Who puts us in right relation to Himself? Who shall come forward and accuse or impeach those whom God has chosen? Will God, Who acquits us?] Who is there to condemn [us]? Will Christ Jesus (the Messiah), Who died, or rather Who was raised from the dead, Who is at the right hand of God actually pleading as He intercedes for us? Who shall ever separate us from Christ's love? Shall suffering and affliction and tribulation? Or calamity and distress? Or persecution or hunger or destitution or peril or sword?

Even as it is written, For Thy sake we are put to death all the day long; we are regarded and counted as sheep for the slaughter.

Yet amid all these things we are more than conquerors and gain a surpassing victory through Him Who loved us. For I am persuaded beyond doubt (am sure) that neither death nor life, nor angels nor principalities, nor things impending and threatening nor things to come, nor powers, nor height nor depth, nor anything else in all creation will be able to separate us from the love of God which is in Christ Jesus our Lord.

Romans 8:31–39 AMP

Notes

Chapter 1: Princess, Why Are You Hiding?

1. Nancy Jo Sales, "Friends Without Benefits," VanityFair.com, September 26, 2013, http://www.vanityfair.com/culture/2013/09/social-media-internet-porn-teenage-girls#.

Chapter 2: But Everyone Is Invited!

1. "Childhood Obesity Facts," Centers for Disease Control and Prevention, page last updated July 10, 2013, http://www.cdc.gov/healthyyouth/obesity/facts.htm.

2. "Teenage Girls Face Another Body Image Obsession," *Good Morning America*, GMA Heat Index, March 25, 2013, http://abcnews.go.com/GMA/video/thigh-gap-surfaces-teenage-girls-image-obsession-18805729.

3. "Going to Extremes: Eating Disorders" infographic, CNN Health, accessed February 21, 2014, http://www.cnn.com/interactive/2012/03/health/infographic.eating.disorders/index.html.

4. "Get the Facts on Eating Disorders," National Eating Disorders Association, accessed February 21, 2014, http://www.nationaleatingdisorders.org/get-facts-eating-disorders.

Chapter 3: Parents Just Don't Understand?

1. Bureau of Justice Statistics, "Family Violence Statistics," U.S. Department of Justice report, June 2005, www.bjs.gov/content/pub/pdf/fvs03.pdf.

2. Gretchen Livingstone, "At Grandmother's House We Stay: One-in-Ten Children Are Living With a Grandparent," Pew Research Center, September 4, 2013, http://www.pewsocialtrends.org/2013/09/04/at-grandmothers-house-we-stay/.

Chapter 5: Is That Any Way for a Princess to Act?

1. Caroline Knorr, "Girls and Body Image Tips," January 14, 2013, Common Sense Media, http://www.commonsensemedia.org/advice-for-parents/girls-and-body-image-tips.

2. S.A.F.E. Alternatives, Schools, accessed February 21, 2014, http://www.selfinjury.com/schools/.

Chapter 6: We Are Family

1. Corrie ten Boom, *The Hiding Place* (Grand Rapids, MI: Chosen Books, 2006), 247. The story can also be read at http://www.pbs.org/wgbh/questionofgod/voices/boom.html.

Chapter 8: Wash Off Those Cinders!

1. "Beauty at Any Cost: The Consequence of America's Beauty Obsession on Women and Girls," YWCA report, August 2008, http://www.ywca.org/atf/cf/%7B711d5519-9e3c-4362-b753-ad138b5d352c%7D/BEAUTY-AT-ANY-COST.PDF.

2. Ross Crooks, "Splurge vs. Save: Which Beauty Products Are Worth the Extra Cost?" infographic, Mint.com, April 11, 2013, https://www.mint.com/blog/consumer-iq/splurge-vs-save-which-beauty-products-are-worth-the-extra-cost-0413/.

3. John Fetto, "How Teenage Girls Spend Their Money," Experian, October 15, 2009, http://www.experian.com/blogs/marketing-forward/2009/10/15/how-teenage-girls-spend-their-money/.

4. "Drug Facts: High School and Youth Trends," National Institute on Drug Abuse (NIDA), January 2014, http://www.drugabuse.gov/publications/drugfacts/high-school-youth-trends.

5. "Drug Facts: Prescription Drugs," NIDA for Teens, accessed February 25, 2014, http://teens.drugabuse.gov/drug-facts/prescription-drugs. See also http://teens.drugabuse.gov/peerx.

6. "Shoplifting Statistics," National Association for Shoplifting Prevention, accessed February 25, 2014, http://www.shopliftingprevention.org/WhatNASPOffers/NRC/PublicEducStats.htm.

Chapter 10: Face Those Fears

1. "Specific Phobia Among Adults," National Institute of Mental Health, accessed February 25, 2014, http://www.nimh.nih.gov/statistics/1SPEC_ADULT.shtml.

2. Thom Rainer, "The Top Ten Fears of Our Youth," BuildingChurchLeaders.com, accessed February 25, 2014, http://www.buildingchurchleaders.com/articles/2005/072605.html.

3. "STEM Careers Demand Risk-Taking; U.S. Teens Fear It, ASQ Survey Says," PRWeb, January 31, 2013, http://www.prweb.com/releases/2013/1/prweb10383378.htm.

4. Bureau of Justice Statistics, "Female Victims of Sexual Violence," U.S. Department of Justice special report, March 7, 2013, http://www.bjs.gov/content/pub/pdf/fvsv9410.pdf.

5. Bureau of Justice Statistics, "Indicators of School Crime and Safety: 2012," U.S. Department of Justice report, June 2013, http://www.bjs.gov/content/pub/pdf/iscs12.pdf.

6. Ibid.

Chapter 11: You Fit Right In

1. "Autism Spectrum Disorders: Data and Statistics," Centers for Disease Control and Prevention, page last updated December 6, 2013, http://www.cdc.gov/ncbddd/autism/data.html.

2. "Attention Deficit Hyperactivity Disorder," Centers for Disease Control and Prevention, page last updated November 21, 2013, http://www.cdc.gov/nchs/fastats/adhd.htm.

3. "What Is Depression?," Depression Health Center, WebMD, accessed February 26, 2014, http://www.webmd.com/depression/guide/what-is-depression.

4. Meghan Neal, "1 in 12 Teens Have Attempted Suicide: Report," *New York Daily News*, June 9, 2012, http://www.nydailynews.com/life-style/health/1-12-teens-attempted-suicide-report-article-1.1092622.

5. Eric Pera, "Two Girls Face Charges in Death of Girl Who Was Bullied," *The Ledger*, October 15, 2013, http://www.theledger.com/article/20131015/NEWS/131019517/0/search.

6. "Teen Suicide Is Preventable," American Psychological Association, accessed February 26, 2014, http://www.apa.org/research/action/suicide.aspx.

7. "Anxiety Disorders in Children and Adolescents (Fact Sheet)," National Institute of Mental Health, accessed February 26, 2014, http://www.nimh.nih.gov/health/publications/anxiety-disorders-in-children-and-adolescents/index.shtml.

Chapter 12: In the Powder Room

1. "Lesbian, Gay, Bisexual and Transgender Youth: An Epidemic of Homelessness," National Gay and Lesbian Task Force, January 30, 2007, http://www.thetaskforce.org/reports_and_research/homeless_youth.

Chapter 13: Where the Boys Are

1. Kristen Armstrong, "Flirting vs. True Attraction," AskMen, accessed February 26, 2014, http://www.askmen.com/dating/heidi_150/165_dating_girl.html.

2. Nancy Jo Sales, "Friends Without Benefits," VanityFair.com, September 26, 2013, http://www.vanityfair.com/culture/2013/09/social-media-internet-porn-teenage-girls#.

3. Ibid., page 3.

4. Yvonne K. Fulbright, "How Teens Really Feel About Pornography," FOXSexpert, FoxNews.com, January 22, 2009, http://www.foxnews.com/story/2009/01/22/foxsexpert-how-teens-really-feel-about-pornography/.

5. Louisa Peacock and Emma Barnett, "NSPCC: 'Girls Think They Have to Act Like Porn Stars to Be Liked by Boys'" infographic, *The Telegraph*, September 3, 2013, http://www.telegraph.co.uk/women/sex/10282145/NSPCC-Girls-think -they-have-to-act-like-porn-stars-to-be-liked-by-boys.html.

6. Jill Bauer and Ronna Gradus, directors, *Sexy Baby* (2012; Two to Tangle Productions).

7. "Teen Births," Centers for Disease Control and Prevention, page last updated August 5, 2013, http://www.cdc.gov/nchs/fastats/teenbrth.htm. See also http:// www.cdc.gov/teenpregnancy/.

8. "About Teen Pregnancy," Centers for Disease Control and Prevention, page last updated November 21, 2012, http://www.cdc.gov/TeenPregnancy/AboutTeen-Preg.htm.

9. Ryan Jaslow, "30% of Teen Girls Admit Real-Life Meeting With Online 'Stranger,'" CBS News, January 14, 2013, http://www.cbsnews.com/news/30-of -teen-girls-admit-real-life-meeting-with-online-stranger/.

10. Jack Maddox, "Police: Texas Teen Flees From Possible Facebook Predator," March 8, 2012, http://www.cnn.com/2012/03/08/justice/texas-teen-flees/?hpt=ju_c2.

Chapter 14: Where Did the Time Go?

1. Benedict Carey, "Where Did the Time Go?," *New York Times*, January 4, 2010, http://www.nytimes.com/2010/01/05/health/05mind.html?_r=0.

Serita Ann Jakes is an inspirational woman of God who leads with wisdom and grace as a noted author, speaker, and visionary. She serves alongside her husband, Bishop T.D. Jakes of the legendary Dallas-based church The Potter's House.

As executive director of The Potter's House Women's Ministries, Mrs. Jakes oversees numerous programs, including God's Leading Ladies Life Enrichment Program and Starting Over. Her passion for the next generation led her in 1997 to launch the nationally acclaimed Distinctively Debutante Program, where girls ages twelve through seventeen are mentored in topics including self-awareness, the strength of femininity, chaste lifestyles, and cultural exposure to the fine arts.

A gifted writer, Mrs. Jakes released her first book, *The Princess Within*, in 1999, followed by *Beside Every Good Man: Loving Myself While Standing by Him* and the novel *The Crossing*. She has also lent her expertise to the stage plays *Woman, Thou Art Loosed* and *Behind Closed Doors* and the film *Jumping the Broom*.

Mrs. Jakes has had the opportunity to share her biblically grounded knowledge with believers and nonbelievers alike through appearances on *Dr. Phil*, CNN, *Oprah's Next Chapter*, and Fox News. She also has been profiled in such notable publications as *Ebony*, *The Washington Post*, *Essence*, and *Rolling Out*.

A loving wife, mother, and grandmother, Mrs. Jakes and her husband have five children and three grandchildren. She finds solace and strength in her faith, family, friends, and the quiet times.